THE COMPLETE GUIDE TO PUGS

David Anderson

Publication Data

David Anderson

The Complete Guide to Pugs---- First edition.

Summary: "Successfully raising a Pug dog from puppy to old age" --- Provided by publisher.

ISBN: 978-1-09326-098-4

[1. Pugs --- Non-Fiction] I. Title.

Design by Sorin Rădulescu

First paperback edition, 2019

TABLE OF CONTENTS

INTRODUCTION

Pugs are one of the most easily recognizable dogs in the world, both because of their wonderfully unique appearance and their incredible popularity. With a lengthy history to rival that of any western-bred canine, Pugs have been a part of Chinese culture for thousands of years. Today, it is easy to see both why they are so popular and why their lives have been so easily integrated into the lives of humans. Charming, compact, cute, and cuddly, these dogs are perfect for nearly any size home and any kind of family. They love to be the center of attention, and they can make nearly anyone laugh.

All it really takes is one look and you know that you are looking at a Pug. They are very short, never reaching the knees of the average fully-grown adult, but they are heavier than they look because they have a lot of muscles. The short, compact size of the dog is probably one of the first two things you notice—the second is the dog's face. Unlike most dogs that have a snout that protrudes from their face, Pug faces are almost entirely flat. The wrinkles on a Pug's forehead stick out as far as his little nose. It is an incredibly distinctive look that makes it impossible to mistake this dog for nearly any other breed.

Given how friendly and affectionate the breed is, it does not take long to integrate a Pug into your home. They are great dogs to have in an apartment or if you have young children because they aren't typically barkers and they tend to love people—even kids. The only thing you really have to watch for is their loathing of being left alone. This is not a dog that you will want to leave home alone too long or too often.

Initially, you are likely to have issues trying to train them because they are not a highly intelligent dog. They do have two significant motivators: food and attention. You will definitely need to be careful about their caloric intake because these are dogs that can easily gain weight, which you definitely need to help your dog avoid. This means transitioning from food as a reward to praise in training as quickly as possible. Fortunately, these dogs love attention, so praise will be nearly as effective.

Pugs are a breed that is particularly sensitive when it comes to temperature. They really do not do well in extreme cold or extreme heat, with extreme heat being detrimental to their ability to breathe. Though you may consider his flat face incredibly adorable, it also makes it more difficult for your Pug to breathe, so you will need to make sure that your Pug never gets too hot.

They can be prolific snorers and they fart a lot, so it is very likely that you will always hear your Pug when he is close by because of the amount of noise he makes when he breathes and as he digests food. They are also prolific shedders, something that often comes as a shock to new Pug parents. Daily brushings are strongly recommended, but considering that your Pug will not mind because he is getting attention, this won't be a particularly difficult task to do every day.

Pugs are very loving, and they are a popular breed all over the world, despite their shedding and noisy breathing. Being such an extremely loving breed that just wants to be wherever you are makes it easy to love them. Owners will need to make sure their Pugs get adequate exercise without overheating, which means you will get to play with them a lot inside your home. This also means that everyone in your family can play and enjoy your Pug, building very strong bonds with your small companion

CHAPTER 1.
Mischievous Charmers – The Defining Characteristics

Photo Courtesy of Brianna Bramato

Pugs have a very distinctive look that makes them nearly impossible to confuse for any other breed. Their appearance is one of the two things that make people love Pugs—the other is their incredibly charming personality. As dogs that adore people, they are easy to bring into any home and acclimate fairly quickly. However, with a dog that has been immensely popular for so long, you have to be very careful about the breeder that you get the puppy from. There are some relatively universal personality traits, but Pugs also come in a very wide range of personalities depending on their ancestors. Talk to 10 breeders and you will find each one will very likely give you a different idea of the breed's basic personality. This chapter looks at the universal characteristics and shared history of all Pugs.

Descriptions and Defining Characteristics

Pugs have a distinctive look that is unmistakable, no matter who their parents are. Their main temperament is going to be relatively similar, with a few variables.

Appearance
Pugs are a small breed with short hair and a very muscular body. Looking at their bodies, Pugs have a lot in common with the stereotypical idea of what a dog should look like, but on a small scale. It's absolutely adorable to watch those compact little frames scurrying to keep up with you—and your Pug will try to keep up as long as you are walking. Those little frames are great for all of the most enjoyable cuddly activities. The Pug is really a lapdog that wants to cuddle up with you and

Multum in parvo,
Latin for "a lot in a little," is the perfect way to summarize the delightful pug. Natural clowns, pugs have a charming sense of humor. They are dignified and committed to pleasing their owners. Their characteristic, distinctive mug and tail are what often draw people to this regal yet fun breed. But, once you let a pug into your life, his personality is what will win you over.

eat anything and everything you are willing to share. You do need to be careful, though, because those small frames cannot take a lot of extra weight, so you will need to make sure that you keep treats to a minimum, and exercise should be done daily. If your Pug looks more like a little sausage than a stereotypical dog, you need to cut back on the treats and add to the amount of daily exercise.

The two most noticeable Pug features are the face and the tail. Some people say that Pugs have humanoid faces, which is kind of true when you consider that most dogs have snouts that jut out quite a ways. Apart from their noses being very different to a human's, there are some very similar features between a human face and the face of a Pug—they are one of those dogs that are much more likely to be compared to their humans than nearly any other breed. Their tails are also adorable and unmistakable.

Temperament

Pugs are an unbelievably adaptable breed, in large part because of how much they love living with people. They will do nearly anything to make sure that you love to have them around and are cuddling up to them.

Most people with Pugs will tell you that they are loveable, charming, and loyal. About half of Pug owners will say that they are fairly easy to train; the other half will tell you that Pugs are incredibly stubborn. Whether or not your Pug is inclined to learning the rules, he is going to want to make you laugh and have fun. If you don't want to spend much time training your little friend, that will be perfectly fine with your Pug. What your Pug wants more than any-

Photo Courtesy of
Julie Bryan

thing is to be a part of the family, to be included, and to follow you everywhere you go.

They are not a breed that does well when left alone. Perhaps your Pug doesn't take it out on your furniture, but there are other things he can do that are undesirable and potentially dangerous. For example, Pugs may go a little crazy when left in a strange place alone, breaking vases and other items in the rooms. Obviously, broken glass is not something you want your Pug to be around, especially if no one is home. Pugs also love to eat, so if you leave food where they can get to it, they will.

Some Pugs are fairly quiet, beyond their very noisy snoring, and others are barkers. You will want to find out which type the parents are from the breeder to get an idea of whether or not your puppy is likely to be loud or quiet. Regardless of whether your dog is noisy, you will have a fantastic travel companion. If you love to hike, your Pug will enjoy it too. If you like going to the park, your Pug will be more than happy to join you. If you are more of a couch potato, that will be perfectly acceptable too. This means that your Pug will easily adapt to your moods and won't be too upset with rainy days at home or with a day out and about. This makes Pugs great travel companions, or lounge-about pooches.

A Distinctive Face and Tail

The face and tail are probably the most recognizable physical aspects of a Pug, so much so that these features have their own section.

Look at the Pug face and you will notice the flat nose, cartoonish eyes, and wrinkles. The eyes look like they take up about a third of the face, making Pugs look more like a cartoon dog than an actual dog. The wrinkles give them an interesting dignity that does not match their clownish personalities. Even people who think that Pugs are ugly find that they typically cannot resist cuddling these dogs, and learn to love those distinctive faces. The coloring on their faces is also very easy to recognize. The ears and face are usually black, while the rest of their body is a lighter color. As they age, the black turns to gray, sometimes making them look like they have spectacles when the graying occurs around the very large eyes.

Their tails are very similar to the tails of pigs and bulldogs. They're cute little swirly tails that look more like springs than tails. Most Pugs can't really wag those tails since they are like springs, but you will see those little springs moving all the same. It is endearing how that face and tail just wiggles when you walk in the door, making it nearly impossible not to cuddle your Pug as soon as you set eyes on him or her.

Photo Courtesy of
Paul Spenceley

Mischievous Little Entertainers With a Strange Dignity

Pugs also tend to be very gentle, which makes them great for families with young kids. You will need to pay a lot more attention to how your child treats the Pug than to how the Pug treats your child. Make sure that your kid or kids are not too rough and don't squeeze the Pug. Your Pug will very likely be more patient than anyone could expect, but you don't want your adorable little pal to be hurt because of his patience with people.

As a breed that adores food, you really cannot leave any food lying around that your Pug can reach. Putting chocolate on the counter is almost certain to result in an unplanned emergency trip to see the vet. Food you leave on the coffee table probably is not going to be there when you get back. Pugs may love you, but they also love food. When you try to get mad at them, they are going to pretend that they don't know why then they will try to make you forget all about it. Unlike dogs like Labs and Golden Retrievers that will appear incredibly remorseful for their wrongdoing, Pugs are much more likely to pretend that they didn't do anything wrong. The more stubborn your Pug, the harder it will be to get him to stop these kinds of actions.

Some breeders will go so far as to say that Pugs are the clowns of the canine world just because of how much they love attention. If it will make you laugh, they are willing to do virtually anything. Since they were bred to be with people, they are very aware of how you feel, and they want you to be happy. This makes them very enjoyable to be with at the end of a long or difficult day.

CHAPTER 2.
Breed History and Characteristics

"Pugs are people dogs. They have been bred for hundreds of years to lay on the laps of royalty for companionship. They are comical and smart, stubborn and playful. Their sole purpose in life is to be around you... and to eat."

Laela Cottone
Thunderstorms Pug Pals

Pugs have an extensive history that is unrivalled by most breeds, and they have been tracked for much of their history because of how integral Pugs were to the people who adopted them. People bred the dogs to be entertaining, cuddly, and a bit mischievous. Though their intellect does not rival that of some other dogs like the corgi, Pugs have always been popular because their charisma and charm make them so endearing. Even without the same intellectual capacity of some of the other popular small breeds, these dogs can learn a lot of highly entertaining tricks, in large part because of their desire to make people laugh. Much of that desire can be attributed to their extensive history with humans.

A Storied History

Photo Courtesy of Karsten & Nikita Engelbrecht

Most dogs become popular because of a movie, TV show, or other type of media exposure, and their popularity is bound to wane after a while. This makes Pugs particularly unique because they have almost always been popular somewhere in the world, even without any PR. A large part of their popularity can be attributed to their small stature and large personality, but these traits are only possible because of the length of time they have lived beside humans, largely as companions.

China in 200 Bc

The earliest recordings of Pugs living with people dates back to 200 BC. They were introduced into Chinese culture during the Han dynasty, which lasted from 206 BC to 200 AD.

It did not take long for this adorable little dog to go from a new breed to a favorite of the most powerful people in China—the emperors and empresses.

Dog of the Emperors

One of the most intriguing Pug features—their very wrinkly face—has always been part of their charm. It makes them look older, wiser, and more distinguished. This is somewhat in contrast to their large, cartoonish eyes, but the wrinkles are certainly a unique feature.

FUN FACT
Exceptional but Not Rare

The dignified pug has a long history, with its roots in China from about 200 BC. Dutch traders introduced the breed to the West via Holland and England. The little pug arrived in Europe in the 1500s where it found favor with royalty. It was not until 1885 that the American Kennel Club (AKC) recognized pugs as part of the toy breed category. The Pug Club of America was founded in 1931, and the breed began to gain status. The pug is not so popular to be common, but not uncommon enough to be considered a rare breed.

It is said that the emperors in China loved this little dog. The combination of their size and personality made them fantastic companions, so they were adopted into the homes of emperors. Pugs became part of the family, not workers as was the case for most dogs adopted by many other monarchies. Pugs would lounge with emperors, empresses, and their families. They were not expected to do anything apart from distract and entertain the family. While some monarchies would use their hounds for hunting and other sports, Pugs were never expected to do much of anything besides be present.

Some people believe that the wrinkles were actually part of the breeding. The Chinese wanted more than just wrinkles; they wanted their dogs to have a more profound statement literally on their face. To some, the wrinkles look like the Chinese symbol for luck, which, if true, has worked as much to be lucky for the Pug as for their people.

This largely peaceful cohabitation between Pugs and China's ruling families certainly played a large role in the development of their personalities. They were so favored that some of the families had guards for their Pugs. With such care and devotion to the dog, it is no wonder they have grown to love being around people, but they do not have unrealistic expectations—mostly they just want to have you around for cuddling and play.

Growing Global Interest

Photo Courtesy of Mandy Saglik

Pugs remained popular in Asia for a very long time, but their popularity really exploded toward the end of 1500s when trade between Asia and Europe became more common. While exchanging and trading a wide range of goods, Europeans were impressed by how personable Pugs were. Around this time, the first Pug made the trip to Europe with a Dutch trader, and the breed was called Mopshond. The Dutch still use this name today for the breed.

Just as it had a meteoric rise in China, the breed gained the attention of royalty in Europe. Looking back over European history, you will find that Pugs were a large part of family life for many of the royal families. They were named the official dog of the House of Orange following an accident. William, who was a prince at the time, was saved when his Pug warned him that the Spanish were advancing. The prince would later become William III of England, and his family brought their Pugs with them from Holland to England.

Marie Antoinette had a Pug before her ill-fated marriage to Louis XVI. Following her execution and the rise of Napoleon, another Pug would become prominent as the pet of Josephine Bonaparte.

Pugs would be reintroduced into Europe later, giving the line a new infusion of genetics. Though it was a much more hostile introduction (the British invaded the Chinese Imperial Palace and took Pugs from the families in 1860), it benefited the Pugs that were in Europe.

Pugs finally made their way to the US around this time. As the American Civil War ended, Pugs provided a welcome note of positivity, although they were not nearly as popular until more recently.

Close Relatives

Though it is not certain exactly how the cute little clown was bred in the early days, it is believed that there is a distant relationship to the Tibetan Mastiff. It is known that the Pug was bred from the Lo-sze, another short-nosed dog in China. It is also possible that the Lion dog and Pekingese could have been used during the breeding of the Pug. There is also some evidence that dogs very similar to the Pug lived in both Japan and Tibet around this time.

Photo Courtesy of Emma Shore

Since Pugs have been bred all over the world, there have been different versions. The Pugs in Europe were from a far smaller genetic pool than the ones in China which existed for hundreds of years. This led to more diversity in the breed, which explains why Pugs are harder to stereotype than most other dogs.

A Unique-Looking Dog that Knows How to Play to a Crowd

The general consensus on Pugs' appearances is that they are cute, even if some people think that they are so ugly they are cute. One of the reasons that people are more willing to overlook their appearance is because of just how affable and entertaining Pugs can be. Perhaps some people feel a bit of sympathy for the dogs, given how you can hear them breathing most of the time, but over time, that can really grow on you. You end up cuddling and enjoying the company of your Pug, and he loves every minute of it. With a buddy that is constantly interested in making you feel better, it is easy for that strange face to end up looking more like a wise soul, despite the evidence of some of the very strange things they may do to get your attention.

CHAPTER 3.
The Ideal Home

Given their small stature and charming personality, Pugs are great canines for nearly any size of home. They don't need much room—your lap is where your Pug will want to spend most of your time together. Between 13 and 18 pounds, you aren't going to have a large dog running around (though they are heavier than you think and can put your leg to sleep if you don't make sure to evenly distribute the weight). They are also incredibly wiggly once they reach your lap, so be prepared for that in the early days, until your Pug learns to settle down and relax.

The one thing to keep in mind is that Pugs are not outside dogs. You should never leave them outside for very long. Pugs are incredibly temperature sensitive, and because of their difficulty in breathing, they really don't do well in heat. You will need to keep this in mind when you are heating your home too.

They aren't the highest-energy dog, but a 30-minute walk every day would be most welcome—as long as you do it during a temperate time of the day. They are not dogs to take on a jog, even if your Pug does tend to bark. Their noses make it too difficult to jog at a human pace, but they are more than capable of walking very quickly with you on a daily walk. They will be more than happy to join you outside for a stroll and then come home and cozy up on the couch for a movie and dinner when you are done.

Best Environment

Pugs are so charismatic and charming that they have always been popular somewhere in the world, often remaining popular (kind of like Retrievers). Their small size means that they can live pretty much anywhere, but their temperature sensitivity means you need to make sure they aren't too hot or too cold. They also are not fans of being left alone for long periods of time, making them a nearly perfect dog for large families where there is almost always someone at home. They are great with kids and can make a single-person home feel a lot more inviting. Getting a Pug is a nearly sure way to bring a great new family member into your home.

Photo Courtesy of Ciahna Heck

A Compact Canine for any Home

Pug frames are adorable and when kept in shape, they have a very muscular frame. With bodies that are essentially a perfectly scaled-down version of a large dog, they can be a great substitute for a large dog. Some of them are barkers, but others tend to be silent, which is what makes it very important to learn about the parents from the breeder if you live in an apartment and don't want your Pug to be too noisy.

Because of their size (less than 20 pounds at their ideal weight), they are lapdogs, but they are much hardier than many other small dogs. This is what makes them so much fun. You will need to be careful about squeezing them, but you can play with them in much the same way you can with a medium-sized dog, and they will love the attention.

It is best to have a fairly small crate for them so that they have a little room for themselves. This is great for both your puppy and an older Pug who wants to have a bit of time alone (particularly if you have a younger dog that wants to play). The crate should be a safe space for your Pug.

Even No Yard Is Fine – Just Make Sure Your Pug Gets Moderate Exercise

Photo Courtesy of Doreen Milone

Your Pug is going to love roaming around the yard with you just as much as hanging around inside the home. If you don't have a yard, that is perfectly fine too. Taking the pooch out for a walk every day is more than enough to keep your Pug happy. This is part of what makes them ideal dogs for nearly any home. Since they were never intended to be working dogs, Pugs don't have the same kinds of energy levels and intellect of many of the other popular dog breeds that bond to humans over their work. Their long history with humans means that they have an understanding of what makes people happy and how to be entertaining. This means they are also accustomed to playing indoors, so long walks or frequent bouts outside are not necessary for your Pug to get adequate exercise. Taking the time to go out for bathroom breaks should be enough if coupled with a 30-minute daily walk and regular indoor play. Your Pug may also appreciate a change of scenery, and both of you will enjoy the fresh air.

Training may or may not be easy, so take the time to understand your pet's personality and abilities to help you decide how much training your Pug will need. That will also help you determine how much time you should spend playing or training your pooch. Your Pug will be perfectly happy either way.

A Warning About Shedding, Snorting, Snoring, and Flatulence

Each Pug is unique, so you can plan for only a few things—they are notorious for being very noisy without intending to be. That is true from both ends.

Their flat noses make it more difficult for them to breathe, so they are very noisy nearly all of the time. You can pretty much always tell when a Pug is nearby because they snort when they are awake and snore when they are asleep. It can be cute, and it is something that you can learn to ignore, or it can come to be its own kind of comfort.

The other thing that Pugs are notorious for is being flatulent. This is in part because of how much they love food (another reason to be careful about their diet). Some breeders actually recommend a diet of high-quality grain-free food. This can help, but we will go into their diet further in a future chapter. For now, keep it under consideration as it can help with this particular problem.

HELPFUL TIP
Home Sweet Home

An ideal house dog, the pug is at home in the city as well as the country. The pug is small in stature and will do well in the homes of city dwellers. Hot, humid climates are difficult for pugs, and they are often difficult to keep trim and fit. This little companion will be equally comfortable around senior citizens and families with young children. Loyal companions, pugs have a large capacity for love and affection.

Considering the fact that your Pug will probably want to sleep with you, keep both of these things in mind to decide if you want them to sleep on the bed with you or in a space close by. At least one of them can be minimized, and the other can be blocked out by some white noise or earplugs.

The final thing that you should be warned about before getting a Pug and that most people do not know is that they are prolific shedders. This seems impossible given their size and short hair, but as one breeder said, "We consider Pug hair a condiment in our household." It is something that most breeders say that they wish people understood beforehand to keep it from being such a surprise. Daily brushings may help (and your Pug will love the attention), but you really cannot stop the shedding. You just have to accept that there will be a lot of dog hair entering your home with that cute little bundle of dog.

Floor Surfaces

Those compact little frames are fairly hardy, but given how much Pugs tend to clown around, you will want to keep your pooch from slipping on slick surfaces or hardwood. Slippery floors, such as laminate and hardwood, are dangerous to all dogs, but particularly to those who tend to mess about, do tricks, and generally play most of the time. Keep your Pug from sliding around by either putting rugs on the floor or adding special mats that are made to stay in place. This will protect your Pug, as well as keeping your family a little safer.

A Natural Lover of Everyone and Everything

Pugs have grown up around people, making them great for any kind of family. Being lovable little cuddle monsters is all they are looking for out of their day, and that makes it very easy to incorporate them into the daily schedule. If you adopt a puppy, it may take a little while for the poor pooch to adapt (they are very fond of those they live with, so leaving their first home may be a bit difficult).

After getting accustomed to your home, your Pug will become an important part of the family. Of course, you will need to keep an adult around during the first few weeks if you have kids, particularly younger children. You may want to introduce other dogs a bit slowly, too, as your Pug may be a little too energetic or eager. It will be highly entertaining later, but you always want to introduce new dogs slowly into your home so that there is less jealousy and tension. It is also about helping to establish good relationships and rules for everyone involved as your new Pug gets accustomed to the new home.

Ideal Lifestyle

As the kind of dog that could inspire an emperor to get it its own guards, it is obvious that these dogs are not made for fighting—Pugs are charmers and entertainers. It is incredibly rare to have a Pug that nips and bites beyond the teething stages (though you will need to train him during this time to ensure he knows it is wrong). Pugs love people and other animals. What you do have to worry about is loneliness. You can't say that Pugs are like shadows because they are far too lively. They are more like personal entertainers that never want to leave your side, so plan to make sure they aren't on their own, even if it means having more than one dog or cat in the family.

Strengths

Pugs are one of the most personable companions you could ever want. Fun and enjoyment to a Pug is pretty much lounging on the couch and enjoying a snack while watching something with you. If you are a couch potato, your Pug will be more than happy to adapt. That does mean you will need to ensure that he gets regular exercise to keep him from putting on too much weight for those little frames (which will help you too).

Pugs can pick up on emotions but tend to want you to be happy. They aren't very likely to mope about if you are down; they are much more likely to try to make you feel better. If you decide that means relax-

Photo Courtesy of Kirsten O'Steen Faulkner

ing on the couch, they will happily relax in your lap and let you pet them instead of making any demands on you. They will work to keep you happy and contented so that they can also be. It is a full-time job, but a challenge that Pugs take on happily.

Common Exercise Benefits

One of the best things about Pugs is that they don't require a lot of exercise. Take them out for a 30-minute stroll every day, and you will both be better off for the fresh air and exercise.

Playing inside to get the rest of your Pug's exercise will be a breeze. It will become an easy way of relieving stress and bonding with your little family member. This helps your Pug to burn off some of the calories while showing your pup that you are happy to reciprocate playtime. You will be as much of a playmate for him as he will be your little clown. Since your dog is not bursting with energy, you won't have to worry about a bouncy dog at the end of the day as long as there are restroom breaks and one walk. Because Pug legs are so much shorter, they will expend a lot more energy on those walks than you will.

Don't plan to jog with your Pug. Even if it will enjoy running at a dog park, it will not be able to join you on jogs. Stick with the walks to keep him from overheating or having a difficult time breathing. The walks alone can help you start establishing a better exercise schedule for yourself.

Beware of Loneliness and Boredom

As has already been mentioned, Pugs are not the kind of dog that do well on their own. They can get very anxious when they are alone and do things that seem out of character. After thousands of years living with people, they are accustomed to being a part of the family and do not understand being left out of whatever fun you are having. They don't tend to be destructive, but that doesn't mean that you won't come home to broken items if you leave them where your Pug can reach them. For example, if you have a vase on an end table next to the couch, that could be knocked over when you come home. You will want to keep these kinds of items to a minimum in your home or when you travel. In the early days, your Pug should probably be in a crate, but over time, you will be able to let him remain free to roam through your home as he learns the rules.

Not Great Learners – Training May Be Rough

Keeping in mind that all Pugs are different, it is likely that your Pug is not going to be the easiest dog to train. Some people have a very difficult time with the house-training; others find it difficult to get them to do tricks. This is because some Pugs are not particularly bright, and others can be incredibly stubborn. This is another thing you will need to learn about the parents from the breeder if you bring a puppy into your home.

Some people have very few problems training their Pugs, so it is possible that you won't encounter any problems beyond the normal issues with your puppy. However, you should be prepared to spend a bit more time training just in case your Pug needs it. With a stubborn Pug, you will need to be very firm so that he learns to respect you.

A Little Dog for Those Who Love Companionship and Training

Pugs are one of the darlings of the dog world because it is easy to love those wrinkly little faces. They look like they are wise but need to be protected. Then you start to get to know your Pug and it will be difficult to imagine life without your new family member.

When you come home, your Pug is going to be ecstatic to see you, and that will make those long, difficult days so much easier to forget. Your Pug will learn what the different looks on your face mean when you walk through the door but will treat you the same way no matter what. If something puts a smile on your face, it is very likely that he will try to use that action frequently to get the smile back on your face.

Once you start to feel more at ease, he will be more than happy to play a game with you, take a walk, or cuddle on the couch. It is really up to you how you want to spend your time; your Pug is just happy that you are there and is ready to entertain you or to just relax.

CHAPTER 4.
Finding Your Pug

"Breeders and foster homes know the personality and temperament of the pug they have, such as energy level and what physical needs, temperament and time requirements the Pug will need. It's important to communicate with your rescue or Breeder what your home, family and lifestyle is like so they can help find the best match for your environment."

Shelley Richfield
Richfield Pugs

HELPFUL TIP
Research and Investigate Breeders

When contemplating purchasing a pug, explore reputable breeders online. A good place to begin your search is the Pug Club of America and local pug breed clubs. Reputable breeders should provide contact information and give references of owners with whom they have placed dogs. Providing a contract and a three-generation pedigree is standard procedure that qualified breeders will willingly comply with. If you are interested in a rescue pug, visit dfwpugs.com for a list of available pugs looking for forever homes.

If you have made it this far, you will very likely be feeling quite excited about a little dog that will be both friendly and cuddly. Pugs will be just as happy to do nothing as to be out walking or doing something exciting. You are going to need to plan for training and socializing your Pug, and you are going to need to be very patient during both of these activities. Your Pug may be stubborn or slow for the training and may be a little overexcited for socializing. In the end, staying with the program will help you have nearly a perfect companion.

We do not recommend that you purchase your new family member from a pet store or online. Do not meet along the side of the road to receive your new Pug. You need to know the history of the parents and your dog so that you and your new friend will enjoy many happy and healthy years together.

Adopting From a Breeder

All purebred dogs come with established health problems that are fairly well documented. Breeders should be well aware of the risks and should be taking precautions to prevent the inherited ailments from being passed along to the puppies. Proper breeding and tracking of the parents can help to breed puppies that are far less likely to suffer from the ailments that are common in Pugs.

Finding a Breeder

The right breeder is one that is willing to take the time to answer all of your questions, provide all of the necessary information, and really take care of the parents and the puppies. They should have as much love for their Pugs as they want you to feel for your new puppy. And they want to make sure that their puppies go to good homes.

The first thing you need to do when looking for the right breeder is to look for someone who clearly loves their dogs and is willing to put in the extra effort and attention to raise them right. They should begin some of the initial training, too, providing training that will prepare the puppies for life. If you find someone who posts regular pictures and information about the parents and the progress of the mother's pregnancy and vet visits, that is a very good sign. The best breeders will not only talk about their dogs and their plans for the parents in the future, but they

Photo Courtesy of
Judi Otto

will stay in contact with you after you take the puppy home and answer questions as they arise. These are the kinds of breeders who are likely to have waiting lists and posts about their puppies and the information their new families provide. The active interest in knowing about what happens to the puppies later shows that they care a great deal about each individual dog.

You will need to plan for hours of research and prepare a list of questions for each of the breeders you talk to. It is likely that for each breeder you call, the conversation will last about an hour. That is for each breeder you contact. If a breeder does not have time to talk and isn't willing to talk with you later, you can cross them off of your list. After you have talked with each of your possible breeders, compare their answers. With a breed like the Pug, there are some variations in personalities based on what the parents are like. If you want a dog that is more easily trained, you want parents that are more intelligent and less stubborn to increase the likelihood that your puppy will be easier to train.

The following are some questions to ask.

- Ask each breeder about the required health tests and certifications they have for their puppies. These points are detailed further in the next section, so make sure to check off the available tests and certifications for each breeder. If they don't have all of the tests and certifications, you may want to remove them from consideration. Good breeders not only cover all of these points, but they offer a guarantee against the most harmful genetic issues.

- Make sure that the breeder always takes care of all of the initial health requirements in the first few weeks through the early months, particularly shots. Puppies require that certain procedures be started before they leave their mother to ensure they are healthy. Vaccinations and worming typically start around six weeks after the puppies are born, then need to be continued every three weeks. By the time your puppy is old enough to come home, the puppy should be well into the procedures, or even completely through the first phases of these important health-care needs.

- Ask if the puppy is required to be spayed or neutered before reaching a certain age of maturity. It is possible that you may need to sign a contract that says you will have the procedure done, which you will need to plan for prior to getting your puppy. Typically, these procedures are done in the puppies' best interest.

- Find out if the breeder is part of a Pug organization or group. Check out Pug Links to see a list of some of the most notable associations and clubs.

- Ask about the first phases of your puppy's life, such as how the breeder plans to care for the puppy during those first few months. They should be able to provide a lot of detail, and they should do this without sounding as though they are irritated that you want to know. They will also let you know how much training you can expect to be done prior to the puppy's arrival in your home so you can plan to take over as soon as the puppy arrives. It is possible that the breeders will start house-training (in which case, you are very lucky if you can get on the waitlist with them). You will also want to find out if they can provide information on how the puppies have been performing and how quickly they have picked up on the training. You want to be able to pick up from where the breeder left off once your Pug reaches your home.

- See what kind of advice the breeder gives about raising your Pug puppy. They should be more than happy to help guide you to doing what is best for your dog because they will want the puppies to live happy, healthy lives even after leaving the breeder's home. You want a caring breeder who is more interested in the health of the puppies than in the money they make. Yes, you could end up paying a considerable amount of money, but you should also get recommendations, advice, and additional care after the puppy arrives at your home. Breeders who show a lot of interest in the dog's well-being and are willing to answer questions during the dog's entire lifespan are likely to breed puppies that are healthy.

- How many breeds do they manage a year? How many sets of parents do the breeders have? Puppies can take a lot of time and attention, and the mother should have some downtime between pregnancies. Learn about the breeder's standard operations to find out if they are taking care of the parents and treating them like valuable family members and not strictly as a way to make money.

Health Tests and Certifications

"ASK QUESTIONS! Be sure to get the name of the breeders Veterinarian. Ask if dogs are kept in the home or kenneled, and if you can visit the parents if both are on site. Ask for references from past buyers. Ask what testing has been done, and will the pups be vet certified before pickup."

Susan Bizier
Rainbow Pugs

Pugs have such a singular and long history that their genetics are very well documented. It also means that they are certain to have a number of genetic issues, though the issues are somewhat different since their history is several hundred years old on two very different continents.

To start, you need to know what kinds of health problems Pugs tend to have. The following are the health tests for Pugs:

- Hip dysplasia evaluations (OFA evaluation)
- Patella evaluation
- Pug dog encephalitis (PDE) DNA test
- Eye examination by someone who is a member of the ACVO Ophthalmologist (they should be registered with either the OFA or the CERF)

Breeders who are members of a Pug association, club, or organization are already showing that they are serious about ensuring their dogs and puppies are healthy. Being a member of a Pug organization necessitates that a set of requirements are being met, so it shows that they are reliable and predictable in the way they treat the puppies.

Contracts and Guarantees

With a breed that has such a varied history and a nearly perpetual popularity, it can be difficult to track all of the genetics. The contracts and guarantees are meant to protect the puppies as much as they are meant to protect you.

If a breeder has a contract that must be signed, make sure that you read through it completely and are willing to meet all of the requirements prior to signing it. The contracts tend to be fairly easy to understand and comply with, but you should be aware of all of the facts before you agree to anything. Beyond putting down the money for the puppy, signing the contract says that you are serious about how you plan to take care of the puppy to the best of your abilities by meeting the minimum requirements set forth by the breeder. Since they focus on your behavior toward taking care of your dog, it is a good sign that breeders want to verify that you are serious about taking care of your puppy. It is probable that the contract will include spaying or neutering the puppy once it matures. It may also say that the breeder will retain the registration papers of the puppy, although you can get a copy of them.

The guarantee states what health conditions the breeder guarantees for their puppy. This typically includes details of the dog's health and recommendations on the next steps of the puppy's care once it leaves the breeder's home. Guarantees may also provide schedules to ensure that the health care started by the breeder is continued by the new puppy parent. In the event that a major health concern is found, the puppy will need to be returned to the breeder. The contract will also explain what is not guaranteed. The guarantee tends to be very long (sometimes longer than the contract), and you should read it thoroughly before you sign the contract. Guarantees are fairly common with Pugs because of how old the breed is. The guarantees state what the breeder is guaranteeing with your new dog. This usually includes information on the dog's health and recommendations on what the pet owner's next steps should be. For example, it may recommend that you take your puppy to the vet within two days of arriving at your home to ensure that the dog is as healthy as it is believed to be. In the event that a major health concern is found, the puppy will need to be returned to the breeder. It will also explain what is not guaranteed. The guarantee tends to be very long (sometimes longer than the contract), and you should read it well before you sign the contract.

In addition to the price of getting your dog, Pug contracts ensure certain behavior by the new human parent of a Pug puppy. Pug contracts usually come with a requirement to have the dog spayed or neutered once the dog reaches maturity (typically six months). The contract may also contain naming requirements, health details, and a stipulation for what will happen if you can no longer take care of the canine (the dog usually goes back to the breeder). They also include information on what will happen if you are negligent or abusive.

Puppy Genetics – The Parents

Good breeders always take the parents' history very seriously and track vet visits and other data points. This is particularly true if the breeder is part of an organization. You will want to review each of the parents' complete histories to understand what traits your puppy is likely to inherit. Pay attention to their learning abilities, temperament, clinginess, and any other personality trait you consider important.

This could take a while, but it is always well worth the time you spend studying and planning for the puppy. The more you know about the parents, the better prepared you will be for your puppy. The great breeders will have stories and details about the parents so that you can read about them at your leisure, as well as get a good feel for the breeders.

Selecting Your Puppy

You want to have a visual of your puppy before you bring your new family member home. See if the breeder will provide videos and pictures so that you can check out your puppy after it is born and as it grows in the first few weeks after birth. You also want to get any data on your dog's vet visits and shots.

Selecting a Pug puppy is pretty much the same as picking any kind of puppy. A lot of it is entirely up to you and what you want in a dog. The ex-

perience can be highly entertaining and enjoyable—and ultimately very difficult. As much fun as it is, you do need to be careful and serious so that you are not swayed by traits that you may find bothersome later.

As you look over the puppies, notice how well each puppy plays with the others. This is a great indicator of just how well your puppy will react to any pets you already have at home.

You also need to look at the puppies as a whole. If you notice that a majority of the puppies exhibit aggressive behavior or seem to tend toward being mistrustful, you may not want to select a puppy from the litter. Similarly, puppies that appear to be terrified of you, such as keeping their tails tucked or shrinking away, are an indication of the kinds of issues you may encounter with your puppy and training. What you want is a litter that is full of friendly puppies, even if they do not start to greet you immediately. Sometimes they just want to play with their siblings or figure out what is happening before acknowledging you.

Next, notice if there is at least one puppy that is very eager to meet you. Many people take that as a sign that the puppy is the right one for their family. However, that is not always the case. Keep in mind that the puppy or puppies that greet you are more forward and demanding than the ones that sit back and analyze the situation first.

The puppies that hang back may be afraid, or, more likely, they just want to understand the situation before they get involved. They are not the alpha types that their eager siblings are. These are your more patient and tame puppies, ones that may be easier to train.

Pick the puppy that exhibits the personality traits that you want in your dog. If you want a forward, friendly, excitable dog, the first puppy to greet you may be the one you seek. If you want a dog that will think things through and let others get more attention, the mellower puppy may be better for your home.

Adopting an Older Dog

The one thing that is universal about puppies is that they are a lot of work. If you miss a day or two of training, it may feel like you are back to square one. Older Pugs can offer you a way to get your Pug without having to dedicate several years to training. You can find older Pugs in shelters, rescues, and even from breeders. Breeders will take back puppies if a person does not treat the dog well or if a person can no longer take care of the Pug for some reason.

Benefits

Older dogs give you more immediate gratification. You don't have to go through those sleepless nights with the new puppy or the endless frustration that comes with early types of training. Older Pugs let you get right into enjoying your dog as you go out on adventures. All intelligent, high-energy dogs require a lot of time and attention as puppies. Bypassing that is a major part of the appeal of older dogs.

Older Pugs not only have the basic training already done, but many of them already know tricks, so you can start exploring the world of what they know and what they still have to learn. This is an incredibly rewarding, funny, and enjoyable experience, just like getting to know a new friend. You can also start your own training. This part is nearly as much fun because older Pugs have the attention span and ability to learn incredibly fast (if they are in the mood), and you will be able to recognize when they are ready to learn and when they are disinterested in the activity.

Better still, they can help you start improving yourself. If you want to get more exercise, an older Pug will help you get started immediately (instead of trapping you in the home, trying to teach it the basics). You also have a wide range in possible activities, and your Pug will be more than happy to join you as you explore new places or get a new look at old ones.

Adult Pugs are ideal for individuals and families who do not have the time or patience to work with a puppy.

Photo Courtesy of Ian Nosek

Rescues

The Pug clubs have their own rescue groups, in addition to their own breeders. You are not as likely to find this breed outside of the small clique because Pug people are very adamant about how the dogs should be taken care of—and they take care of their own. Pugs that you get through organizations and breeders have most of the necessary information that is required to sell puppies, meaning you will have the medical history and vaccination information on the dog (although if the human parent was negligent or abusive, the medical history and information may not have been tracked while the dog was with them).

It is very easy to contact the organization to see about adapting an adult Pug. They will require you to apply for the adoption simply because they want to ensure that the dog gets a great home—a place where the dog will be able to live out the rest of his or her days. They will also try to match you up with an adult dog who is ideal for the environment you offer and the lifestyle you live.

Warning About Socialization

Because Pugs are small dogs, you may be overprotective and your Pug could suffer from small dog syndrome. He may be more timid or aggressive based on how you treat your Pug. Early socialization ensures that Pugs are happy and remain comfortable around other people.

Pugs that are not properly socialized at an early age can show signs of aggression as they age. This could present itself as nipping, lunging at people, growling, and barking. Barking is not always a problem, but the other behaviors are definitely habits you want to avoid. By making play-dates for your Pug puppy, you will be able to start helping him learn to be happy and excited about meeting other dogs and people instead of feeling a need to intimidate them. Mostly this intimidation reflects your Pug's own anxiety and fear because the Pug is not accustomed to being around new people or dogs.

It is also possible that a Pug will be aggressive when you return home after being away. He could feel abandoned or unhappy about your disappearance. This is behavior you will also need to discourage, and is part of the reason adults should always be around during those first few weeks after your Pug arrives.

CHAPTER 5.
Preparing for Your Puppy

Those months, weeks, and particularly the days before your new Pug arrives are incredibly exciting. Before you get too carried away though, you should take the time to focus and get your home fully prepared for your new canine. It will take you about the same amount of time to puppy-proof your home as it does to childproof it, so you should plan to spend a good bit of time and money preparing before the new family member arrives. Perhaps it isn't the most enjoyable aspect of having a dog, but it is definitely worth the time and effort you put into it. Making sure your new Pug has a safe space with all of the essentials (especially the toys) will make his arrival a great time for everyone—especially your new canine companion.

Photo Courtesy of Judi Otto

Preparing Your Kids

Pugs are absolutely adorable, but they are not nearly as hardy as they look. To make sure that everyone has a great time, you need to make sure your children understand how to play with the Pug in a way that won't potentially cause harm to your cutie. You can actually begin to prepare your kids as soon as you decide to adopt a Pug—no matter what age the Pug is. You will need to take a different approach to preparing a toddler than a teen, but there are many aspects of the preparation that are universal.

Be prepared to refresh these points with your children periodically before the puppy arrives, as well as the day your Pug comes home. When your kids begin to play with the puppy f or the first time, you must be present to monitor the entire time they are interacting with your new family member. Remember that you will need to be very firm to make sure that the puppy is not hurt.

The following are the five golden rules that you want to make sure your children follow from the very first interaction.

1. Always be gentle. Those little Pugs are absolutely adorable, but they are also fairly fragile, despite their sturdy appearance. At no time should anyone play rough with the puppy (or any adult Pug.)

   This rule must be applied consistently every time your children play with the puppy. Be firm if you see your children getting too excited or rough. You don't want the puppy to get overly excited either because puppies may end up nipping or biting. It isn't their fault because they haven't learned better yet—it is the child's fault. Make sure your child understands the possible repercussions if they get too rough.

2. Chasing is an outside game. It can be easy for children to forget as they start to play and everyone gets excited. That short game of getting away can quickly devolve into a chase, so you will need to make sure your children understand not to start running. Once they get outside, chasing is perfectly fine (though you will still need to monitor the playtime).

   Running inside the home is dangerous for two primary reasons. It gives your Pug puppy the impression that your home isn't safe inside because he is being chased, or worse, he will hurt. Or your puppy will learn that running inside is fine, which can be very dangerous as he gets older. One of the last things you want is for your Pug to go barreling through your home, knocking people off their feet, because it was fine for him to do that when he was a puppy.

3. Always leave the puppy alone during mealtime. This is true whenever your puppy is eating (this can apply to when your kids are eating

Photo Courtesy of
Nate Novicki

as well since you don't want your Pug to get accustomed to eating people food when your kids are eating). You don't want your Pug to think that anyone is trying to take the food away. Pugs aren't typically aggressive, so it isn't likely they will nip or bite because someone is near their food. However, they can feel insecure about eating if they feel like someone may take their food, which is obviously not fair to your Pug. And older Pugs can be a bit more protective of their food, which could lead to some conflicts. Save yourself, your family, and your Pug trouble by making sure everyone knows that eating time is your Pug's time alone.

4. The Pug should always remain firmly on the ground. This is something that will likely require a good bit of explaining to your children as Pugs look a lot like toys, especially Pug puppies. No one should be picking the puppy up off the ground. You may want to carry your new family member around or play with the pup like a baby, but you and your family will need to resist that urge. Kids, particularly, have trouble understanding since they will see the Pug more like a toy than a living creature. The younger your children are, the more difficult it will be for them to understand the difference. It is so tempting to treat the Pug like a baby and to try to carry it like one, but this is incredibly uncomfortable and unhealthy for the canine. Older kids will quickly learn that a puppy nip or bite hurts a lot more than you would think. Those little teeth are incredibly sharp, and you do not want the puppy to be dropped. If your children learn never to pick up the puppy, things will go a lot better. Remember, this also applies to you, so don't make things difficult by doing something you constantly tell your children not to do.

5. All of your valuables should be well out of reach of your children, even your teens. Valuables are also not something you want to end up in the puppy's mouth, but that is almost guaranteed to happen if you leave jewelry where someone can easily pick it up. Teenagers are just as likely to grab whatever is within easy reach to play with the puppy, so they are nearly as much of a threat to your valuables as tweens and kids who are older than toddlers. If your kids get curious, they are not likely to stop to consider if they should be doing something because they want to know what will happen if they use something to play with the puppy. The end result will be an incident that will certainly not make you happy, nor your children when you get upset with them. If you don't want your puppy or children to destroy something valuable, make sure it is never easily accessible.

Preparing Your Current Dogs

"When introducing your current dogs to your new puppy: allow them to sniff and get to know each other, but watch closely. The other pets may feel left out with all the attention the new dog gets."

Caryn Mullin
Wild Bunch Kennels

If you already have a dog, you are going to need to plan to prepare that canine or canines for the introduction of another canine companion. Start by teaching your kids the rules, then turn your attention (and that of your kids, if they are old enough) to preparing your current furry companions. The approach you take with a dog is completely different than what you do with children because you are not going to be explaining rules—you are going to let them know that you still love them.

Here are the things you can do to help ease the transition to having a new Pug around the home.

- Think about your dog's personality to help you decide the best way to prepare for that first day, week, and month. Each dog is unique, so you will need to consider your dog's personality to determine how things will go when the new dog arrives. If your dog loves other dogs, this will probably hold true when the puppy shows up. If your dog has any territorial tendencies, you will need to be cautious about the introduction and first couple of months so that your current dog learns that the Pug is now a part of the pack. Excitable dogs will need special attention to keep them from getting overly excited when a new dog comes home. You don't want them to be so excited they accidently hurt the new Pug.

- Consider other times when you have had other dogs in your home and how your dog reacted to these other furry visitors. If your canine displayed territorial tendencies, you are going to need to be extra careful with how you introduce your new pup. If you haven't invited another dog to your home, you need to have a couple of playdates with other dogs at your home before your new Pug arrives. You have to know how your current furry babies will react to dogs in the house so you can properly prepare. Meeting a dog at home is very different from encountering one outside the home.

- Think about your dog's interactions with other dogs for as long as you have known the pup. Has your dog shown either protective or possessive behavior, either with you or others? Food is one of the reasons that most dogs will display some kind of aggression because they don't want anyone trying to eat what is theirs. Some dogs can be protective of people and toys too.

You should have a place specially designated for your puppy too. This is where the puppy will sleep, eat, and spend the day when you cannot give him your full attention. This should be an area where no other dog can go either. Make sure that none of your other dog's stuff is where your puppy will spend the majority of the time. You don't want your dog to feel like the puppy is taking over his territory. This means setting up the area in a space that doesn't include your current dog's favorite bed, couch, or other items. Make sure your children understand never to put your dog's stuff in the puppy's area as well.

When it comes time for your dog to meet the puppy, you will need to do that away from home to ensure that territorial instincts do not kick in. Plan ahead with neutral ground where the dog and puppy will have their first encounter. This gives them a chance to get to know each other before entering the house together.

When you go to introduce your dog and puppy, make sure you have at least one other adult with you. It is best to have the whole family if possible, but having at least one other adult means that there is someone to manage each canine. If you have more than one dog, then you should have one adult per dog. This will make it easier to keep everyone under control. Even the best dogs can get overly excited about meeting a puppy. One of the people who needs to be there is the person who is in charge in the home (or people, if you have more than one person in charge). This helps establish the pack hierarchy.

HELPFUL TIP
Be Prepared!

The introductory time could take a while, depending on the personality of your dog. The friendlier and more accepting your dog is of the puppy, the easier it will be to incorporate your new puppy into the home. For some dogs, a week is enough for them to start feeling comfortable together. For other dogs, it could take a couple of months before they are fully accepting of the new pup-

Get organized before you bring your puppy home. Know how to puppy-proof your dog's new environment well in advance of your pug's arrival. If this is your first pet, research what your puppy will need to successfully acclimate to your home. The proper size crate, nontoxic water and food bowls, and puppy food recommended by your veterinarian are among the basics you'll need to welcome your new family member.

py. Since this is a completely new dynamic in your household, your current dog may not be pleased with you bringing a little bundle of energy into his daily life. This is enough to make anyone unhappy, but especially a dog that has grown accustomed to a certain lifestyle. The older your dog is, the more likely it is that a puppy will be an unwelcome addition. With their abilities limited, older dogs can get cranky around puppies who don't understand the rules or don't seem to know when enough is enough. The goal is to make your puppy feel welcome and safe while letting your dog know that your love is just as strong as ever.

The same rules apply, no matter how many dogs you have. Think about the personalities of all of them as individuals, as well as how they interact together. Just like people, you may find that when they are together, your dogs act differently, which you will need to keep in mind when they are around the puppy. The introduction may need to be done with one dog at a time so that you do not overwhelm the puppy. Introducing each dog, one at a time, will help them calm down a bit before bringing all of the dogs together at the same time.

Your dog and the puppy will need to be kept apart in the early days (even if they seem friendly) until your puppy is done with vaccinations. Puppies are more susceptible to illness during these days, so wait until the puppy is protected before the dogs spend time together.

Dangerous Foods

Dogs digest foods differently to humans, and there are a number of things that are safe for people to eat that are dangerous to dogs. Most people know that dogs shouldn't have chocolate, and many have heard that grapes are on dogs' Do Not Eat List, but there are a lot more than just those two foods.

The problem is that your Pug is going to think that whatever you are eating is just fine for everyone in the family. However, there are a lot of things that go into people food that definitely should not be given to Pugs. Given their small stature, it does not take as much to harm a Pug as it takes to harm a larger dog (though none of these foods should be given to any dog since they hurt dogs of all sizes). The following is a list of foods that you need to make sure your Pug can never get to as they are potentially fatal if consumed by a dog.

- Apple seeds
- Chocolate
- Coffee
- Cooked bones (they can kill a dog when the bones splinter in the dog's mouth or stomach)
- Corn on the cob (it is the cob that is deadly to dogs, corn off the cob is fine, but you need to make sure that your Pug cannot reach any corn that is still on the cob)
- Grapes/raisins
- Macadamia nuts
- Onions and chives
- Peaches, persimmons, and plums
- Tobacco (your Pug will not know that it is not a food and may eat it if left out)
- Xylitol (a sugar substitute in candies and baked goods)
- Yeast

In addition to these potentially deadly foods, there is a long list of things that your dog shouldn't eat for health reasons. The Canine Journal has a lengthy list of foods that should be avoided. It includes foods like alcohol and other things that people give dogs, thinking it is funny. Remember that dogs have a very different metabolism and the effect that these foods have on them is much stronger than the effect they have on people.

For the sake of your Pug's health, it is best just to keep all of these foods out of reach, even if the items are nonlethal.

Hazards to Fix

Just as there is a lengthy process for preparing your home for a baby or toddler, you have work ahead of you to get your place puppy ready. Since Pug puppies are so small, they can get into so many things that really are not safe. For the month or three leading up to your puppy's arrival, you are going to be puppy- proofing your home. It is going to require a considerable amount of time, so make sure you set aside at least a month (more time is better) to get your home puppy-ready. The time you put into making your home safe for the puppy is well worth any extra effort.

This section details the areas of the home where you should really focus your attention to make sure you don't miss anything important that could be dangerous for your little darling.

Also, be aware that Pugs (puppies in general) will try to eat virtually anything, even if it isn't food. Nothing is safe—not even your furniture. Puppies will gnaw on wood and metal. Anything else within their reach is fair game. Keep this in mind as you go about puppy-proofing your home.

Kitchen and Eating Areas

Easily the most dangerous room in the house, the kitchen is a combination of poisonous foods, dangerous items, and poisons. It is the room where you should probably plan to spend most of your time when puppy-proofing your home. Everything you would do to protect a small child in this room is something you will need to do for a Pug. This could include making sure the cabinets are locked in case your Pug is clever enough to figure out how to open them. He is going to be following you around like a little shadow once he is allowed out of the puppy area, and he will be learning that things open. Some Pugs are clever enough to be able to get into cabinets, especially the cabinets where you do not want them to go.

You will need to make sure that all poisons are put in places where your Pug cannot reach them (whether in the kitchen, in other rooms of the house, the garage, and all outdoor areas). Pugs can get into nearly everything, and they will be exploring a lot when given the opportunity. Anything that may catch your attention or draw your interest is worth a try—that's what centuries have taught them. Being vigilant about making sure they can't hurt themselves is vital to keeping your Pug safe. At no time should you leave poisons in an unsecured place in your kitchen,

Trash cans are equally dangerous because that's where all kinds of great smells exist to lure your Pug to misbehave. Having just gone over the list of foods that they shouldn't eat, having any of these foods in the trash is a serious risk to a Pug puppy. There are also things like poisons, plastics, and other items your puppy may think should be taste-tested. Just because your Pug is small does not mean that it is impossible for him to knock over a trash can. Take all of the necessary precautions, such as getting a trash can you can lock or storing it under a cabinet that is locked. This will keep your puppy from getting into too much trouble or creating a mess for you to clean up.

All electrical cords need to be up and out of reach of little Pug puppies that could be curious as to what cords are and how they work. You don't want the puppy to trip or get tangled in a cord any more than you want your puppy to try to eat the cord. Then there are things like blender cords and other wires that connect to heavier items that you don't want pulled on top of your puppy. Cords aren't just electrical either—if you have long cords for your blinds, these need to be shortened or put where they will not fall to the floor where your Pug can reach them.

Bathroom and Laundry

The dangers in the bathroom are almost the same as those in the kitchen, just in a smaller space. There are so many poisons in bathrooms that keeping the doors closed could be the best way to go. Since that is really not an option for many families (particularly if you have children or teenagers who are likely to forget), you need to make sure to keep everything that could attract attention or pose danger locked up or out of reach.

Keep the toilet seat closed, and don't use any automatic cleaners. Some Pugs are clever enough to learn how to drink out of toilets, which means it is up to you to keep the toilets inaccessible to your curious pup. If the toilet seat is left open (as is bound to happen occasionally), make sure there aren't any poisons in it by avoiding having any automatic cleaners in the water.

Though it doesn't seem likely at first, the laundry room can actually be a dangerous room as well. The easiest way to deal with it is to keep the door shut if you can. Many families keep a number of miscellaneous items (including poisons) in the laundry room because it is kind of a catch-all place. You may only have bleach, laundry detergent, dryer sheets, and other clothing cleaners, but even those can be very dangerous to a Pug. This is particularly true of items like laundry pods. You also need to keep all dirty clothing off of the floor—if for no other reason than to keep your Pug puppy from dragging the most embarrassing garments all around your home. There is also a chance that your Pug may try to eat some of the clothing, which would not be great for your Pug. Nor is it a great time for you as you have to take an emergency trip to the vet's office or animal hospital.

Other Rooms

Most of the other rooms of the house should be relatively safe since people don't tend to keep chemicals outside of cabinets.

You will need to do a thorough inspection for cords that are low to the ground or within jumping distance of your Pug's reach. All of these will need to be secured well above where your Pug can go. Don't forget about spaces like the computer area and entertainment center where there is typically a lot of wiring. You will also need to check the window cords to make sure they are too high for your puppy to reach.

All cleaning products need to be stored someplace that your puppy cannot go, too. If you keep objects like air fresheners on counter surfaces, make sure that these areas are not places where your Pug can go. Since most Pugs are allowed on couches and beds, you will need to clear off end tables and nightstands—and anything accessible from the furniture that contains chemicals.

If you have a fireplace, all cleaning supplies and tools will need to be stored in a place where the puppy cannot get into them. The area where the fire is also needs to be made inaccessible to curious puppies. This needs to be true all of the time so that your puppy does not play in the ashes or with the wiring in the fireplace.

If you have stairs in your home, they will need to be cordoned off so that your puppy cannot try to go up or down them. Tables (including end tables and coffee tables) need to be cleared of dangerous objects, such as scissors, sewing equipment, pens, and pencils. All valuables should be kept in safe locations away from furniture where your puppy will go.

If you have a cat, you are going to need to keep the litter box off the floor. It needs to be somewhere that your cat can easily go, but your Pug cannot. Since this could include teaching your cat to use the new area, it is something you should do well in advance of the puppy's arrival. You don't want your cat to undergo too many significant changes all at once. The puppy will be enough of a disruption—if your cat associates the litter box change with the puppy, you may find your cat protesting the change by refusing to use the litter box.

Garage

The best way to deal with the garage is to make sure your Pug cannot go into it. There are so many dangerous things in garages that keeping puppies out is the best policy. However, given their size, it is certain that the little Pug will manage to slip into the garage when you don't expect it. With all of the chemicals, sharp implements, and other dangerous tools that are stored there, the garage is one of the most hazardous places in any home. Never leave your Pug alone in the garage, even when it is an adult. It is likely that your puppy will be in the garage when you take car trips, which is why it is important to puppy-proof it.

All items related to your car and its maintenance have to be stowed high off the ground where your puppy cannot go, and a locked area is the safest way to store them. This includes all lubricants, oils, and cleaners, as well as wrenches and tools. You will need to do the same for all of your lawn-maintenance items, bike tools, and anything used for heavy machinery or that includes chemicals.

Puppies will chew anything, including tires, cans, tools, and bags. Everything that can be placed up high or locked in a cabinet should be.

You will need to do this with all of your hobbies too. Things like fishing tackle are incredibly dangerous and should be stored somewhere out of reach, too. You will need to make sure there is nothing hanging over the countertops where the puppy can try to pull it down.

The best way to tackle the problem is to enter the garage from a toddler's perspective. Anything that you would immediately move for a toddler should be moved for your puppy. Get down low and see the garage from your puppy's perspective. If you keep your cars in the garage, you can move them out to get a better view. Move anything that could be a potential danger.

Outdoors and Fencing

Your puppy should never be outside alone because there are too many hazards, even after you puppy-proof it. Keep in mind that you should never have your puppy outside of the designated puppy area without constant supervision. This is just as true in your yard as it is inside your home. Even if you have a fence, your puppy should not be left unattended when he is outside.

Puppy-proofing the yard won't be nearly as time-consuming as puppy-proofing the inside. This doesn't mean that it isn't just as important though, especially if you plan to play with your puppy in your yard. Plan to spend between an hour or two outside inspecting and cleaning up in preparation for the arrival of your puppy.

Begin by inspecting the fence to make sure there are no breaks, holes, or other potential problems. You will also need to look for areas that dip under the fence that would be easy for a dog to make bigger. Make sure to have all problems with the fence repaired and fill in holes under the fence. You want to make sure the cute little puppy can't escape and given its size, it won't take much for him to slip through or under the fence.

Determine where in your backyard you want your puppy to go to the bathroom. You will want to make sure this area is cleared of all potential dangers because your puppy is going to be spending a good bit of time in the spot every day. All poisons and dangerous tools need to be stored elsewhere, such as in a shed or a secure place in the garage. If you have objects like a birdbath or other artificial structures in the puppy's bathroom area, move them somewhere else. Of course, it is easiest to select an area that is already open and close to the door for rainy, hot, or cold days. It will be easier to maintain an area that is already clear.

Choose a different area in the yard for your puppy to play. Having a place for play and a place for going to the bathroom is important because you want the Pug to focus on using the bathroom in one place, and not be distracted by trying to play with you. This also lets your Pug know that it is time to play when you go to the different

spot, which will make your little puppy that much more excited. Give this area the same inspection that you gave the house-training space.

Stroll around the rest of your yard to look for other chemicals and dangers. All of them should be moved somewhere that you can secure them. Even with dedicated places for using the bathroom and playing, your Pug is probably going to go to other areas of the yard, particularly if you have children. Make sure there is nothing dangerous in the entire yard.

Make sure all of your current plants are safe for dogs. Puppies will just as happily chew on plants as toys, making it essential to ensure there is nothing that can harm them.

Secure all water sources, such as pools, ponds, and streams. If you have a firepit or grill, make sure it is secure so that your puppy cannot access anything potentially dangerous.

Just like the garage, inspect your yard as if you were a toddler. Keep your eyes open for anything that could be interesting to a Pug, then determine what is too dangerous to remain.

Supplies and Tools to Purchase and Prepare

Planning for the arrival of your puppy includes buying all of the necessary supplies, like a crate, food, toys, and brushes. Start buying these things a month or two before your puppy arrives so that you can break up the cost over time. Bringing home a puppy can get very expensive; spare your budget by breaking the expenses up over a long period of time.

- Crate
- Bed
- Leash
- Doggie bags for walks
- Collar
- Tags
- Puppy food
- Water and food bowls (sharing a water bowl is usually okay, but your puppy needs his or her own food dish if you have multiple dogs)
- Toothbrush
- Brush
- Toys

Feel free to add anything else you think of or want to have when your puppy arrives. Health-care items like flea treatments can be purchased (they are expensive), even though you won't be able to use them for a while. Puppies should not be treated until they reach the specified age.

Planning the First Year's Budget

The budget for having a puppy is a lot more than you would think—it's still less expensive to bring in a puppy than a new infant. You will need to have a budget, which is another reason to start purchasing supplies a few months in advance. When you buy the items you need, you will begin to see exactly how much you will spend a month. Of course, there are some items that are one-time purchases, such as the crate, but many other items you will need to purchase regularly, like food.

You also need to have a budget for the one-time purchases. This means doing some research ahead of time for those purchases. It is almost guaranteed that you are going to overspend, but you want to stick to the budget as much as possible.

Begin budgeting the day you decide to get your Pug puppy. The cost will include the adoption cost, which is typically higher for a purebred dog than for a rescue. If you want to rescue a Pug, you should figure out where you want to find your newest family member. Plan to spend a lot of time researching costs for bringing your puppy home, as well as the other costs.

The vet and other health-care costs should be included in your budget. Regular vaccinations are required, and an annual checkup should be included in the budget. Vet prices vary a lot between different states, even between cities, making it difficult to average the cost. It is always worth the cost, but you want to know what it will be before your puppy arrives.

There are a lot of activities that you can do with your dog. Pugs are great pets because you will pretty much always want to enjoy your Pug without ever leaving home. A simple Google search yields pages of recommendations on ways to entertain and be entertained by your new family member. The Pug community is worldwide, and people who have Pugs tend to adore their dogs and are constantly thinking of new ways to enjoy the company of their canine companions.

Keep Things Out of Reach

"Puppies are like toddlers, they will get into everything."

Cindy Jones
Cjsmunchkinland Pugs

Pugs are going to right there with you wherever you go, which means that they are going to be able to get to nearly everything within your reach. It is very important to keep a lot of things out of their reach, especially for the times when you are not home. They can knock things over, like plants and decorations. Pugs can have anxiety issues, and they may knock things over while trying to look out windows to see you.

The Puppy Area

When you set up an area for your puppy, it needs to be in a place that won't disrupt your current routines, especially for other pets. It would also be best to have an area where it will be easy to clean the floors. Your puppy is going to have a lot of accidents in those early days, and you don't want to have nice carpeting, rugs, or flooring ruined. It should also be close to where you sleep unless you want to set up two puppy areas, one for the day and one for the night. Breeders also recommend that it be somewhere a bit quieter so that it isn't too overwhelming for the puppy in the early days.

Most breeders also recommend safety gates and fencing. You will need to test it to make sure that your puppy can't get out, and other animals and children cannot get into the area.

There should not be any furniture in the puppy's area either. Given puppies' penchant to chew anything, you want to make sure that the only thing constantly in their reach is their puppy paraphernalia. A few safe toys, water, bedding, and maybe a blanket that is difficult to tear up should be the only things in the puppy area.

CHAPTER 6.
The First Week

Everything is going to change the day your cute little Pug comes home with you. Years later, you will still remember just how things played out as your newest family member came barreling into your home like a little pack of personality on four legs. Like a jester, your Pug is usually going to be the center of attention whenever he is in the room, and nearly everyone will love playing with or cuddling up to such a charming little mischief-maker. Every puppy is a bundle of possibilities that requires a lifetime commitment from you to help the puppy reach his full potential.

That first week is critical to the development of your Pug as it helps to establish the dynamic in the home and to make the puppy begin to feel safe in a new environment. These are the early days of seeing your Pug reach his full potential. With all of the puppy-proofing already done, you now have the daunting task of assisting your little Pug in learning how to play, where to go to the bathroom, and finding out that the new home is a great place to live. This is when you really get to learn about the joys of having such a personable dog in your home.

Preparation and Planning

Just like you have to prepare your home and yard, you have some final tasks to do before your new puppy enters the home. You should start with completing a final check of your home to make sure everything is still secured. Everything should be set up for your puppy too. From the puppy area to food and toys, you should have everything set and ready for your puppy. Anything that you can do before the Pug's arrival will help you to better enjoy your time together when he gets there so that you don't have to try to do stuff on the fly—you are going to have to do that enough without leaving too many things to do for later. Start inspecting your home to make sure you didn't miss anything.

You should do one more inspection from the ground level in every room of the house and the garage. This should be done a few hours before the puppy arrives to make sure that all of the risks have been removed (habits can be difficult to break, so make sure everything is in order). Make sure everything is properly puppy-proofed.

During the final week before the puppy arrives, create a list of everything that your puppy needs for the first day. The following should help you get started:

- Food
- Bed
- Crate
- Toys

- Water and food dishes
- Leash
- Collar
- Treats

Verify that you have everything on the list out and ready for use before your Pug walks through the door. You don't want to have to run out and buy them after the puppy is home, partly because you want those things readily available, and partly because you don't want to miss time with your newest family member and want to get started establishing a routine.

If you plan to have a fence to keep the puppy penned into a specific area of the home, have the gate set up and verify that it cannot be knocked over or circumvented. Your Pug puppy is probably going to try to make a break for it if there are any weaknesses or holes in the fencing around his designated area because your Pug is likely to try to get out to stay with you as much as possible.

Set up a schedule for the puppy's care. Know that the plans are going to change, but you need to have a starting point. This will ensure that people complete their assigned tasks and help to make your puppy

HELPFUL TIP
Now What?

Once you've made the all-important choice of the perfect companion and new family member, be patient with your pug. His car ride home should be in the crate you've purchased for him, not too big or small. The first week in his new home is the perfect time to get your pug accustomed to your touch. Handle him gently, stroke his ears and tail, touch his paws, and get him used to being brushed. When your pug is in the crate, don't bother him. Allow plenty of time for your pug to get used to you and his new home.

feel safe—dogs prefer structure, so schedules are a great source of security for them. Tweak the schedule as it becomes clear that changes are needed, but try to keep it as close to the original schedule as possible. Having a schedule in place before the puppy arrives will make it a lot easier than if you try to establish something after the arrival. The Pug is going to have more than enough energy to keep you busy, making it difficult to make a plan after his arrival.

The schedule should include a bathroom break after every meal. There is a good chance your puppy will need to go then, and this will help establish where the right places are to use the bathroom.

Have a final meeting with all of the family members to make sure all of the rules are remembered and understood before the puppy is a distraction. Children will need special training in how to handle the puppy, and you are going to need to be very strict in making sure they aren't too rough with the pup. Verify that your children understand that they are not allowed to play with the puppy unless there is an adult supervising them. Determine who is going to be responsible for primary puppy care, including who will be the primary trainer. To help teach younger children about responsibility, a parent can pair with a child to manage the puppy's care. The child will be responsible for things like keeping the water bowl filled and feeding the puppy, and a parent can oversee the tasks.

Pug training happens from the moment your puppy is given into your care. The rules and hierarchy should start to be established from that first car ride home.

As tempting as it is to cuddle and try to make your Pug feel comfortable, you will need to put the Pug in a crate for the ride—you cannot start by making an exception. Your puppy is learning from the very beginning. Remember, this is a breed that has been living alongside humans for a very long time, and they know how to take cues from you. Anything that they can do to make you drop your guard and let them get away with stuff, they are going to use later. As difficult as it will be, you will need to be firm and consistent with your Pug puppy.

The Ride Home

Two adults should be present on the first trip. Ask the breeder if the puppy has been in a car before, and, if not, it is especially important to have someone who can give the puppy attention while the other person drives. The puppy will be in the crate, but someone can still provide comfort. It will definitely be scary because the puppy no longer has his mom, siblings, or known people around, so having someone present to talk to the puppy will make it a little less of an ordeal for the little guy. Pugs may not tend to lean toward being fearful dogs, but that doesn't mean that they don't get scared.

Photo Courtesy of Kirsten O'Steen Faulkner

This is the time to start teaching your puppy that car trips are enjoyable. This means making sure that the crate is secure instead of being loose to be moved around during the drive. You really don't want to terrify the puppy by letting the crate slide around while the puppy is inside it, sitting helplessly. This kind of jostling will teach your Pug that cars are terrifying instead of making him feel safe.

Digestive Issues

The first day to first week is likely to be difficult for your puppy, and for Pugs that often manifests as digestive issues. Your puppy may have diarrhea or constipation, which will make him cry more. This is normal for the first day, but consult the breeder if you have concerns. If it lasts for a couple of days, ask your vet during the first visit to make sure everything is all right.

First-Night Frights

"When puppies leave their littermates they are scared and lonely. They may whine at night. This is something that can take about a week before puppy quits his or her whining."

Cindy Jones
Cjsmunchkinland Pugs

That first night is going to be incredibly scary to your little Pug puppy. Away from mommy and any siblings, as well as the humans the puppy has come to know at the old home, it is understandable if the puppy is terrified. As understandable as this may be, there is only so much comfort you can give your new family member. Just like with a baby, the more you respond to cries and whimpering, the more you are teaching a puppy that negative behaviors will provide the desired results. You will need to be prepared for a balancing act to provide reassurance that things will be all right and also keep your puppy from learning that crying gets your attention.

You should have a sleeping area established for the puppy prior to the arrival. It should include a bed, and probably a crate or pen. The entire area should be blocked off so that no one can get into it (and the puppy cannot get out) during the night. It should also be close to where people sleep so that the puppy does not feel abandoned.

Things like sounds may attract your puppy's attention, and those unfamiliar sounds can be scary. If you can minimize the number of noises, this could help make the first night a little less terrifying. These noises may not be as noticeable to you, but dogs have a much better sense of hearing.

To make things a little more familiar, you could also request that something that smells like the mother be provided. The best way to get an item that smells familiar is for you to send a blanket along that the breeder can place with the mother for a few days before the puppy comes home. The blanket can then also travel with the puppy in the car on the way to your place.

Your puppy is certainly going to make noises over the course of the night, and you cannot think of them as an inconvenience (no matter how tired you are). The puppy is sad and scared, so you will just need to endure it. Do not move the puppy away from you, even if the whimpering

Photo Courtesy of
Julie Bryan

keeps you awake. Being moved away from people will only scare the puppy more, reinforcing the anxiety and fear of your home. Doing this on the first night will make the wrong impression, starting things off on the wrong footing. Over time, simply being close to you at night will be enough to reassure your puppy that everything will be all right.

Not getting much sleep should be something you expect during that first week or so (just like with an infant), but especially that first night. Make sure you don't have work or anything pressing the next day so that the lack of sleep isn't too disruptive. Losing sleep is part of the deal of bringing a puppy into your home. Fortunately, it doesn't take as long to get a puppy acclimated as it takes with a human infant, so your normal schedule can resume more quickly.

You will need to learn to ignore the whining, but that will get easier over time so that the puppy doesn't learn to do this every night. If you give in, over time, the whimpering, whining, and crying will get louder. Spare yourself the trouble later by teaching the puppy that it won't work.

Do not let your puppy into your bed that first night—or any other night until he is fully house-trained. Once a Pug learns that the bed is accessible, you cannot train him not to hop on it. If he is not house-trained, you are going to need a new bed in the very near future.

The last thing that is going to cut into your sleep is the need for regular bathroom breaks. You can set up something in the puppy's space, or you can plan for trips outside every few hours (depending on how you plan to train your puppy). Whatever house-training path you use, you are going to need to keep to a schedule even during the night to train your puppy where to use the bathroom. Puppies will need to go to the bathroom every two to three hours, and you will need to get up during the night to make sure he understands that he is always to go to the bathroom either outside or on the wee pad. If you let it go at night, you are going to have a difficult time training him that he cannot go in the house later.

First Vet Visit

This is going to be a difficult task because you may feel a bit like you are betraying your puppy (especially with the looks your puppy will give you during shots and the following visits to the vet). However, it is necessary to do this within the first day or two of your puppy's arrival. You need to establish a baseline for the puppy's health so that the vet can track progress and monitor the puppy to ensure everything is going well

Photo Courtesy of
Joseph Mallozzi

as the Pug develops and ages. It also creates a rapport between the Pug and the vet, which can help too. The initial assessment gives you more information about your puppy, as well as giving you a chance to ask the vet questions and get advice.

It is certain to be an emotional trip for your Pug, although it could be exciting in the beginning. Wanting to explore and greet everyone and everything is going to be something that your puppy is very likely to want to do. Both people and other pets are likely to attract your puppy's attention. This is a chance for you to work on socializing the puppy, though you will need to be careful. Always ask the person if it is all right for your puppy to meet any other pet, and wait for approval before letting your puppy move forward with meeting other animals. Pets at the vet's office are very likely to not be feeling great, which means they may not be very affable. You don't want a grumpy older dog or a sick animal to nip, hurt, or scare your puppy. Nor do you want your puppy to be exposed to anything potentially dangerous while still going through the shots. You want the other animal to be happy about the meeting (though not too excited) so that it is a positive experience for your puppy.

Having a positive first experience with other animals can make the visit to see the vet less of a scary experience, and something that your Pug can enjoy, at least a little. This can help your puppy feel more at ease during the visits.

The Start of Training

Your Pug's training begins the moment your puppy enters your car or your home, and it will continue for most of your Pug's life. The first few weeks will have some more intense training as you are teaching the basics, and this will serve as the foundation for all other training. The focus during these first few weeks is to minimize undesirable behavior.

Barking

Some Pugs are quiet; others are rather vocal. If you want your Pug to be less vocal about everything, you must start during that first week when your puppy barks. It will probably mean a few extra treats, but that is how you will teach your Pug what "quiet" means. However, avoid giving your puppy treats during the first week. There are good odds that his tummy will be a little upset; don't compound that by giving him extra food. Your puppy will also be noisy when trying to get your attention, so you will be training yourself to react in a certain way to the noises as well.

The Leash

Leash training will probably be pretty easy since your Pug will be excited about anything that you want to do together. The training is actually just as much for you as for the puppy. You do not want to get used to dragging the puppy away from things that the Pug is sniffing. You will need to start finding ways to keep your puppy walking without being too forceful.

Given how excitable Pugs are, many breeders recommend that Pugs be trained to walk with harnesses. Your pup probably has not used one before, so there may be a learning period when he has to get accustomed to using a harness instead of being able to move around freely like he does at home (his boundaries are marked by walls, doors, and gates, not something on his little body). Don't drag your puppy because that will make your puppy dislike walks. Instead, you can let the little puppy explore parts of your house while being supervised and wearing the leash. You will need to keep an eye on your puppy the entire time that you let him drag the leash around so that he doesn't get hurt or choked.

Teaching Respect

Respect is a part of training, even for a dog as affable as the Pug. Whatever behavior you teach now will be lessons that your Pug carries forward. You want to teach your puppy to respect you without fearing you. Consistency is the best way to do that. Do not make exceptions during the first week because you will be fighting that lesson essentially for the rest of your Pug's life.

Grooming – They Are Constantly Shedding; Get Used to Regular Grooming

They may be small in the beginning and their hair short, but Pugs are an unexpectedly prolific shedding breed. Their fur will get into everything, including your food, shower, containers, toothbrushes, and nearly anything else in your home or car. You will love your Pug, which means you will get acclimated to it. Just be aware that you are in for a lot of fur everywhere.

One thing you can do to reduce the amount of fuzz around your place is to make time to brush your Pug often. If you want to make it a daily task, your Pug will love it, and you will have fewer fur tumbleweeds rolling around your home.

CHAPTER 7.
The First Month

Photo Courtesy of Rhiannon McGuinness

Following all of the trials, tribulations, excitement, and changes of that first week, you will probably have a routine mostly established. You will also very likely be tired after a week of learning so much about your puppy and having such a major change to your normal routine.

By now, you probably have a pretty good idea of your puppy's personality and what works to motivate your puppy best (praise is easily the best way to get a Pug to act, but food is a very close second).This will make the first month a bit easier than the first week, and by the end of that month, you will have a much better idea of how to progress with training and playtime.

At this stage, your Pug will seem adorable and cute, which may make you drop your guard a bit. Don't be fooled, because you must continue to be firm and consistent in your approach so that the training sticks. Some Pugs can learn quickly, others are fairly slow, but none of them will do what you want them to do if you don't take a firm and consistent approach to training. Training should also be done daily, if only for short periods of time to get your pup used to the idea of training. You should see some results of the training by the end of the month, although the results may not seem very big. Small steps must be taken to get your puppy to be the perfect companion.

Not Up to Full Strength

As much fun as you want to have with your puppy, that adorable little jester still has a limited supply of energy. You won't be able to go on long walks, let alone hikes with your puppy. The activities will need to be tailored to a puppy still learning about its abilities, mostly at home. There will be walks on leashes, but that is still largely a learning experience. If you have a yard, that can also be a great place to play. Still, most of your trips will be within a block or two of home.

Walks will need to be kept short and exercise to short periods of time, though you can have many exercise sessions over the course of the day. Typically, the exercise sessions will end with a nice puppy nap, meaning you won't be overly tired but will have time to do things you need to do without feeling like your puppy misses you. The puppy will still need to sleep in the designated puppy area because when that little pup wakes, you may not be in the room.

By the time the month wraps up, your puppy will have a lot more stamina. Over the course of the month, and subsequent months, you will need to adjust your schedule to accommodate longer walks and playing sessions. Longer exercise sessions mean fewer sessions, which can actually free up more time in your schedule. Just make sure to monitor your Pug's energy levels so that you aren't pushing for too long a walk or play session.

Photo Courtesy of Noel M. Lehmkuhl-King

Setting the Rules and Sticking to Them

"Puppies need a consistent routine. They need a confined space and should not be allowed to roam the whole house right away. Puppies need lots of praise and reassurance especially the first few weeks."

Bonny Allegro
HoneyPugs

Photo Courtesy of
Amanda Dawn Williams

Pugs love to be with you, but they do prefer to do things that they enjoy, with minimal work. Since they are so cute and affable, you are much more likely to give in, thinking that you can train them later. This is something that your Pug is going to notice and use to get his way. Although you may feel that your puppy is too young for a firm approach, this is something you will need to fight against. Puppies need a firm approach, perhaps even more so as you are establishing a baseline. Exceptions to the rules should never be made in the early days if you want the training to stick.

By failing to keep your training consistent, you are setting yourself and your Pug up for a lot of contention since it will be difficult to convince your dog that you are serious. Inadvertently, you have already taught your Pug that listening to you is optional. With the right look or action, the Pug can get you to lose focus.

Remember, they are mischievous, so training is important to keep them from hurting themselves or destroying your items.

A firm, consistent approach with your Pug is best for both of you. You want to have fun together, but that also means making sure your Pug knows that there are some things that are required, including listening to you.

If you can manage to be firm and consistent over that first month, things could get a bit easier in the subsequent months. Keeping a level head and applying the rules without any exceptions paves the way for easier training going forward. There will be a trust and respect that is built up from being a great trainer who keeps all of the lines clear, making the rest of your time with your Pug so much more enjoyable.

Early Socialization

Pugs love to be surrounded by others, whether it is by other dogs or people, but that doesn't mean they don't require socialization. It will be far easier to socialize with your Pug than it is with many other breeds though, as long as you plan for it. A socialized Pug will be a fantastic companion that can enjoy nearly every situation and make people in the family feel better at the end of a long day.

Pugs are not known for being aggressive, but there could be triggers that make them agitated. Failing to socialize a Pug could result in an aggressive Pug or one that can be a little terror in your home. Aggression in Pugs is often a result of fear, so if you do not socialize your Pug, you could be setting the dog up for an unhappy life where he fears other people and dogs. Aggressive Pugs tend to jump on people, bark, nip, and growl, which can be scary to other people and dogs despite the Pug's size.

HELPFUL TIP
Getting to Know You

Your pug's personality will begin to make its appearance in the first month. You'll probably have fallen head over heels in love with your new companion, but this is the time for consistently sticking with a definite schedule. Keep to your regular feeding, walking, and socializing agenda. Being firm yet kind with your pug puppy is the route to a well-mannered and loving pet. Positive attention will guide your pug. Always try to be patient.

Some of them can also be territorial, which you can stop early by setting up playdates for your Pug with other dogs. If you have friends or other family members who have dogs, have them bring their dogs over to help train your Pug that other people and dogs are fun and exciting, and should be welcomed into the home if you are around when it happens.

Toward the end of the first month, you can also start to socialize your Pug during the walks. This is best to do while having people with dogs visiting, or friends who want to join you. If you encounter a calm, friendly dog with people who are willing to let their dog say hello to your puppy, this can help your Pug learn to be less wary on walks too. You will want to make sure that the dog is friendly, and that the people are all right with the encounter—do not just go up to the other dog without asking first.

Your Pug will also need to be socialized with people. This should be fairly easy because people are going to want to meet your puppy while you are out walking. Do be careful when you let people meet your Pug because you want it to be a positive experience for everyone. Anyone who wants to meet your puppy will need to follow the same rules. The puppy should not be picked up—all play should be with the Pug's feet firmly on the ground. Children should be kept as calm as possible so that they do not get carried away and be too rough with the puppy. The point of socialization is to help the puppy feel happy and excited about meeting new people and dogs, instead of teaching him that there are reasons to be afraid of leaving home.

It is too early to take your puppy to a dog park. The first month is all about learning more about the home and immediate area and meeting people and dogs your pup is likely to encounter regularly. Your puppy also needs to finish all of the vaccinations before having a lot of exposure to other dogs, especially off the leash. All socialization should be in an environment that you can control. Dog parks are barely-contained chaos with the excitement and enthusiasm of dogs enjoying the freedom of being with other dogs.

You will need to be extra kind to older dogs and pets that you have in your home at this time. The puppy is definitely a strain on them for so many reasons. Have time in the schedule just for you and your older dog so that your dog doesn't feel that you don't care about him anymore. It will probably be best to keep older dogs and puppies apart for most of the first month.

Treats and Rewards vs. Punishments

"Pugs are VERY food motivated, but can overeat easily. Treats can make training much easier."

Susan Bizier
Rainbow Pugs

Training and treats are so closely thought of together that it can be difficult to consider anything else as an effective means of training your dog. Second to treats, people think of punishment as a way of dissuading dogs from undesirable behavior. Although these have been the typical methods used in training, there are serious problems with both, particularly with Pugs. Teaching a puppy proper behavior is a balancing act to make sure that you are firm, but not cruel, so you should provide rewards, but use something better than food.

As Pugs are real people-pleasers, positive reinforcement is the most effective way to train them. Food is an obvious choice, but you have to be very careful not to overfeed your puppy. You don't want the little pup to get accustomed to eating too much, especially as he will become an adult and will no longer have a rapid metabolism. Starting with treats is best, but you should quickly begin using praise and extra petting as the primary form of positive reinforcement. You could even add some extra playtime after a training session if your puppy does very well.

Having your puppy's respect is also essential for successful training. If your Pug respects you, it will be much easier for him to accept positive attention instead of treats because he will know you are in charge.

You may occasionally need to resort to punishment with your Pug, particularly if he nips or chews on furniture. However, you have to be careful not to train him to believe in things or actions that will make your life more difficult. Never use the crate as a place to punish your Pug—it should be a safe haven when your puppy wants to be alone or sleep. It is not a jail, and you should not treat it as one. You can use time out instead to get your point (and disappointment) across to the puppy. It should be somewhere that the puppy cannot interact with you, no matter how much the dear barks, whines, or whimpers, but you should still be visible to your pup. You don't want to scare the puppy. The point is to let him know that you are still there but are intentionally not interacting because of the puppy's actions. By denying him access to you without you disappearing, you are reminding him just why he needs to behave.

Exercise – Encouraging Staying Active

"Pugs can use a daily walk or play at a local dog park or play date with a pal a few times a week. They do not need a huge amount of exercise to stay healthy, but walks are great for them and keep their food in check."

Laela Cottone
Thunderstorms Pug Pals

Even if your puppy can't take long walks during the first month, the little pup still needs to get rid of a lot of energy. You will quickly realize just how sedentary you have been if you did not have a dog before because you will be on the move almost all of the time the puppy is awake.

Exercise will be fairly simple during the first month. Taking short, frequent walks while your Pug gets accustomed to the harness and leash will help you prepare for longer walks as much as it prepares the puppy. Playing will be a lot easier because you don't have to harness the Pug up. You can strike a good balance between walks and play in the early days to help keep your puppy expending his energy.

Other people and dogs can be great helpers when it comes to puppy training—especially adult dogs. Things are much easier for the puppy to understand when an adult dog does it first.

Make sure that the leash is a good fit. Your Pug probably isn't going to be able to break it (unless it is an old, frayed leash), but Pugs can be incredibly fast when it comes to working off collars and leashes and taking off. You can bring this up with the vet to make sure the harness is properly secured for your Pug.

Fun Pug Activities

In terms of the kinds of activities that you can do with your Pug, pretty much anything that you want to teach your Pug is fair game. This is a breed that wants only to be with the pack having fun—all of the time. If you aren't playing, your Pug will be perfectly content to rest in your lap while watching TV or playing games. Pugs don't really care as long as you do it together.

Do keep in mind that they are not as hardy as they look, and make sure everyone is careful during play time.

As mentioned in a previous chapter, a quick Google search yields pages of information and recommendations of activities you can do with your Pug, whether it is rainy, cold, hot, or sunny outside. The Pug community loves to share the joys of having a Pug, so it is always a great idea to look for new things to do with your Pug.

Pugs will play tug of war until you decide to quit. You will need to make sure everyone understands not to sling the little dog around, particularly on slippery floors. However, some good steady pulling will keep your puppy very happy and wanting to play more.

Fetch is another game that Pugs will play with little prodding. Once they realize that you want the toy back so that they can chase it down again, you will have a game that conserves your energy while expending the puppy's.

There are also puzzle games that Pugs can thoroughly enjoy. Most of them won't figure out the puzzles quite as quickly as breeds like Corgis and German shepherds, but they will definitely get there much faster than most other small breeds. Pugs not only love fun, they adore food, so puzzle games that involve food are a favorite for the breed.

CHAPTER 8.
House-Training

"Be diligent and patient when potty training, and be prepared for it to go on for up to a year."

Melissa Standish
Moonstruck Pugs

HELPFUL TIP
A Consistent Routine

Your pug will become used to his scheduled routine. If you put in the time and effort to maintain your part of the house-training bargain, you will be rewarded. Your pug should be taken outside to relieve itself 10-15 minutes after eating. This is the time to get your dog accustomed to being on a short leash. Take him to approximately the same ten-foot square area each time he goes out to "do his business." Praise your dog once he has finished relieving himself in the appropriate area. Remember to use treats in moderation. Pugs tend to become overweight as they age. Kind words and affection can work as effectively as treats.

It is one of the least enjoyable aspects of having a puppy, but house-training is essential to raising that puppy. With Pugs, you are in for an unpredictable ride (though the breeder should be able to tell you about how long it took to train the parents to give you an idea of how long it could take you to complete the training with your puppy).

Two rules should be followed during this time.

1.   Your puppy is not to be left to roam the house free when no one is around to monitor the puppy. Your Pug won't be pleased with the idea of being in a soiled crate, so that is a deterrent from using the bathroom when you are not around.

2. Your puppy should have constant, easy access to the locations where you plan to house-train. If you cannot provide this, you will need to have frequent trips outside as your puppy learns.

Once you have your training plan, be prepared to enforce all of the rules and restroom schedule. You have a few decisions to make to help you better prepare and plan for the task ahead of you.

Understanding Your Dog

Every Pug is different, so you are going to need to work with your puppy as an individual to figure out what works best. It may take a while before your puppy understands just what you want in those early days because it is an entirely new concept.

Consistency is key with all dogs, no matter their personality. Food is a great motivator, but you need to stick with small treats, or a piece of kibble to keep the puppy from overeating. As your puppy shows signs of being motivated by seeing you happy (for example, he gets excited when you do or reacts by wanting to play when you talk), start using praise as much as treats to reinforce the puppy using the bathroom in the right place.

You will need to tailor the schedule to your puppy's needs. To start, always plan to take the puppy outside to the bathroom after eating and sleeping. If you successfully get outside right after these, you have a much better chance of getting the puppy to the right place to do his business.

Key Words

All training should include key words, even house-training. You and all members of the family should know what words to use when training your dog where to go to the bathroom, and you should all be using it consistently. If you have paired an adult with a child, the adult should be the one using the keyword during training.

It would be best to watch a few videos providing some hints and tips on training and the words that are often used. You have to be careful not to select words that you use inside the home because you don't want to confuse your puppy. Selecting the right word is a lot trickier than you might think because you use some of the words in conversation more often than you might expect (particularly if you are potty training a child at the same time).

Inside or Outside

Eventually, you are going to need to train your Pug to use the outside only, but depending on the time of year and your individual Pug, it may be necessary to start inside. In the middle of a snowstorm is not the time to be teaching your puppy that outside is required. This will make it far more difficult to train your Pug. Be aware that if you have to start inside, you are going to need to purchase extra pads so that you don't run out.

You will also need to expedite the timeline to train your puppy where the only acceptable places to go are in the home.

If you are able to start outdoor training, know that you are going to need to go out every two or three hours—including the middle of the night. After a few weeks, you will be able to go out less frequently, but in the beginning, the best way to train is by going out a lot so that your puppy learns to keep all business outside.

Puppies (and most dogs) tend to use the bathroom after waking up and after eating their meals. Even if it is out of the schedule, make sure you take your puppy out during these times because it is very likely the little guy will need to go. This will make it a bit easier to train if you are telling your puppy to do something the Pug wants to do.

If you have an area chosen for the restroom, teaching is easier. The Pug will begin to associate that area of the yard for one purpose. When you get there, the expectation will be easier to understand than if you let the puppy sniff around and go anywhere in the yard. It also makes it a lot easier to clean up the yard as you won't have to hunt for where the puppy went—it's all in one place.

Leashes can help in the early days too. If you gently lead the puppy to the area, it will become obvious over time that the Pug should go there to use the bathroom, and then playing might be in the cards.

Establish Who Is Boss – Kindly But Firmly

As difficult as it is, you have to take a firm, consistent approach, no matter how cute the puppy. Fight the urge to consider something good enough or close enough. Your Pug needs to use the designated area and learn to hold it when inside. This won't happen if you make exceptions. Pugs watch you for cues, and if you send mixed signals, your Pug is going to opt for what is easiest.

Positive Reinforcement – It's About Respect

"Pugs do best with positive reinforcement. They need to go to the bathroom generally right after waking up and right after eating, so those are good times to take them out. The younger a puppy is the more often it needs to potty. Adult Pugs tend to go about 4 or five times a day"

Shelley Richfield
Richfield Pugs

Positive reinforcement works incredibly well for Pugs, even the puppies. Take a few pieces of kibble with you when you are teaching your puppy where to go. Learning that you are the one in charge will help teach the Pug to look to you for cues and instructions. He may try to push you a bit, to convince you that it's okay to let things slide because he wants to enjoy time with you and not be forced to do something.

While you are being firm and consistent, when your puppy does the right thing, you also have to lavish the little pup with praise. This is just as effective because Pugs love to see their people happy. They want to hear that they are good, and if you give them an extra treat or kibble, this will put them over the moon.

Knowing what you want will make it easier for the Pug to start to do things the way you want them done. By focusing on this aspect, you are establishing the respect needed for all future training.

Punishing your Pug is strongly discouraged. All punishment does is train your Pug not to do something when you are around or to do it where you won't find it. The lesson you are trying to teach is not the one your Pug learns, so it is best to stick with positive reinforcement—that

Photo Courtesy of
Ciahna Heck

he understands very well. Training a Pug (or any dog) is not exactly like teaching a human, and you cannot take the same approach.

Regular Schedule, Doggie Door, or Newspaper

The last decision you need to make is how you plan to conduct the training. A good bit of the decision will be based on what you have already considered. Your Pug is likely to need to go to the bathroom after the following activities:

- After waking (both after naps and after night)
- After spending two or three hours in a crate or his puppy area
- After eating
- While walking

Watch your Pug for cues and to determine what activities make the little pup have to go. Start tailoring your schedule around your puppy's unique needs.

Puppies have small bladders and little control in the early days. If you have to train inside, there needs to be a single designated space, and you need to stock up on appropriate pads for the puppy to have somewhere to go that isn't the floor. The pads are better than newspaper and can absorb more. You will need to plan to transition as quickly as possible before the Pug learns that inside is acceptable—this will be incredibly difficult to retrain later if you let him go inside for too long.

When out for walks, it is the perfect time to train your puppy to go. Remember, you can use a leash in the backyard to help get the idea of walks and potty across a little clearer.

It's All on You – Many Pugs Aren't Quick Learners

Pugs love to make you happy, but not all of them are not the quickest learners. You could be in for a long training regimen when it comes to getting your Pug to always go outside, or you might be lucky and have your Pug take to it rather quickly. Regardless of how quickly your Pug learns though if you aren't firm and consistent, your dog is going to feel that inside your home is an acceptable place to use the bathroom.

CHAPTER 9.
Socialization and Experience

As an incredibly sociable breed, Pugs are one of the easiest dogs to socialize, and they should be socialized early to help them keep that nearly unlimited potential to love everyone and everything. Pugs are fun when they play the jester and try to keep everyone laughing; not when they are scared, nervous, or upset. You want your companion to be comfortable everywhere the two of you go, and that is the ultimate goal of socialization.

Despite how easy it is to socialize a Pug, you still have to plan for it. Without planning and a controlled environment, socialization can go very wrong, very quickly. If you keep things simple and under control, your Pug will learn to relax and enjoy the company of other people and dogs.

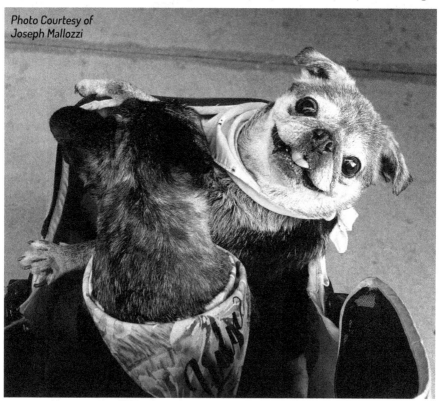

Photo Courtesy of Joseph Mallozzi

*Photo Courtesy of
Ian Nosek*

Benefits of Socialization

HELPFUL TIP
A Brand-New World

Socializing your pug properly is an important part of being a pet owner. Daily walks will help your pug become familiar with people, other dogs, the mailman, cars, and bikes. Keep your puppy on a short leash during this initial phase of socialization. Encourage his curiosity, but don't push him into stressful or frightening situations. The "sweet spot" for puppy socialization is 3-12 weeks of age. Beyond the four- month mark, socialization can become more difficult. Do not be discouraged, however. You can teach an old dog new tricks with patient and consistent guidance.

It is always important to socialize dogs, but even more so with small dogs. People are inclined to being overprotective and cautious with small dogs and puppies, and this can lead to serious problems later. The benefits of early socialization are that it can make things that much more enjoyable for everyone involved, no matter what the situation is. A socialized dog will approach the world from a much better place than a dog that is not socialized.

Problem Arising From Lack of Socialization

Socialization starts the moment your puppy arrives. Without socialization, no amount of training is going to help your Pug better interact with other animals and humans. All other rules still apply during socialization, so keep that in mind while you help your dog meet new friends.

If you treat your dog like a doll or infant, protecting it from everything and everyone, the dog is going to develop small dog syndrome; even a breed as notoriously personable as the Pug can develop it. They need to be allowed to learn how to interact with others so that they aren't always terrified or upset with you when there are other people or dogs around them. It isn't healthy for your Pug to always be anxious or nervous around others, especially when you can easily avoid it. Make time to socialize your puppy to make his life enjoyable and so that he is as happy to meet new people and dogs as you and your family are.

Why Genetics Matter

Genetics are important in terms of not only the dog's health but his personality. Pugs don't tend to be aggressive or unpleasant, but there are always exceptions. Early socialization can help bring out the Pug heritage of loving new people, dogs, and experiences. You will want to learn

Photo Courtesy of Evie Vorpagel

whether or not his parents are skittish or standoffish so you will know what to expect and can watch for those traits and correct them.

Some Interesting Training

Pugs may or may not be easy to train, depending on what kind of learners they are. Since they tend to pick up their behavior from others, you can use peer pressure to your advantage. If your Pug sees you reacting positively to another dog's tricks, your Pug is very likely to try to do the same tricks to get the same reaction from you. Early socialization can help develop a positive relationship with other dogs so that you can show your Pug new tricks that he has watched other dogs do and your Pug will learn to do them.

Common Problems

Pugs don't typically have problems as long as they are socialized from an early age. They love almost any living creature if they learn not to be afraid when they are young. However, they can develop small dog syndrome if you don't take the time to introduce them to others early. They can be real terrors if they are uncomfortable around others.

Properly Greeting New People

It can be a lot of fun, so it isn't something most people avoid. (Who doesn't love meeting and playing with a lovable little dog?) The difficult part is finding the time to do it often enough to reinforce the positive behaviors and teach the puppy that the world is a fun place to live in.

Greeting new people is usually a pretty easy task outside of the home, but it can be a bit tricky when you are at home. Training your Pug how to treat visitors may take a little longer because he will very excited and will want to be the center of attention. In the end, it is worth the effort as your Pug becomes an enjoyable companion for you and anyone who visits.

Photo Courtesy of Mandy Saglik

Behavior Around Other Dogs

Pugs are incredibly agreeable dogs. They do not need to be alphas, but they can believe that things should always be fun and exciting. If you have an older dog, most Pugs will be able to peacefully work out who is alpha and who isn't without too many problems. Since Pugs hate to be alone, it is probably better to have another dog if you are absent from the home for several hours every day.

CHAPTER 10.
Being a Puppy Parent

You can spend a lot of time just playing with a puppy, especially a Pug puppy. The world looks entirely different as you see the world as everything is surprising and new to your puppy. The new perspective helps a lot, but there is a lot of work too. Having a puppy is incredibly fun and tiring.

Pugs are gregarious and love to play. Getting them to take things seriously can be a bit trying at times because they just want to play or lounge. If you are not consistent and firm, they are going to take away the idea that you can be plied to have fun instead of focusing on work and training.

A well-trained Pug is one of the best companions you could ever have. It may take a while to get there, but it is more than worth the effort in the end.

Staying Consistently Firm

HELPFUL TIP
Puppy Parenting 101

Your intelligent pug will be playful and affectionate but can be mischievous and stubborn on occasion. Do not leave your pug alone or unattended for long periods of time. Encourage your pug's flexibility but not his aggressiveness. Dedicate yourself to your young pug, and remain consistently firm and caring. School your puppy in the proper ways to greet strangers and other dogs. The hours you spend with him in these early months of his life will be well spent.

You have to be firm and consistent when training any puppy, but the Pug is a unique challenge. It isn't that he is trying to outsmart you or be the one in control—he just wants to play. All the time. It is easy to give into that desire, but you can't, especially in the early days. Once you get in the habit of letting your puppy get away with something, it will be very difficult to train him to take you seriously later. He's a puppy, and that means maintaining the same approach to training all of the time. No exceptions.

Your puppy doesn't mean any harm when trying to gnaw on you, but you have to teach that biting is wrong. It won't be nearly so cute lat-

er if he bites someone while trying to play. If you can gain his respect, you are still going to have your work cut out for you. It will be a lot easier though, as he will learn to listen to you when you use your training voice or no-nonsense voice.

What to Watch for in Misbehavior

Pugs tend to have great personalities, but that doesn't mean they are perfect. There are a few personality traits that you will need to watch for in your puppy.

Pugs tend to know what they want. This has earned them the reputation as a stubborn breed, and it can make training a bit more difficult. Establishing a great bond and earning the puppy's respect will go a long way to making your puppy more willing to listen. Since he loves being with you, as long as you make it clear that he needs to listen, stubbornness probably won't be too much of a problem.

Expect your dog to beg. Pugs love their food about as much as they love people. From the very beginning, you must make sure that no one in the family or who visits gives your Pug food unless it is dog food or treats. He should never be fed food from a person's plate. Giving in once will make your Pug that much more prone to begging. Make sure that begging never results in success to avoid problems.

Photo Courtesy of
Lam Cao

Your puppy may also have high energy levels in the early days. You will want to stick to the schedule, making sure your puppy gets enough walking and playtime. This will not only burn off energy, but it can be used as a way to start training. A well-trained Pug can do almost anything, and a few minutes of browsing Pug tricks online can give you a wealth of ideas on what will keep your Pug active and learning.

Managing Gnawing and Chewing

All puppies will gnaw on anything they can get their little mouths around. Initially, they chew because of teething; chewing helps sooth the pain. They will gnaw on people or other animals as they learn how to play. It should be fairly easy to teach a Pug not to chew on items or people, but you will need to be firm and consistent.

While your puppy is teething, you can give the little pup ice cubes. This not only gives him something to gnaw on, but the cold will help soothe the pain. Keep everything you don't want chewed out of reach, including furniture.

For the first few months, keep the puppy in his designated area and keep everything he shouldn't chew out of that area. Toys and other items can be left in the area for your puppy to chew when you are busy.

*Photo Courtesy of
Katherine Van Nort*

Photo Courtesy of Paul Spenceley

When outside the area, you will need to monitor the puppy's behavior. If the puppy starts to chew on something you don't want him mouthing, give him something that is acceptable to chew. Don't take your eyes off your puppy. As soon as you do, your little Pug is very likely to chew on anything in reach. If you can't keep a constant eye on the puppy, put the little guy back in the puppy space until you can.

Playtime!

Playing with a Pug is easier than waking up in the morning. All you have to do is move around and talk to prepare your dog for having a good time. Pull out a toy to get your pup really excited.

Spend a bit of time looking through everything that people have taught their Pugs. Those little jesters are more than happy to learn to jump through hoops, play fetch, and pretty much anything else you can devise. Their strength is in entertaining and spending time with you. Use that to find things that you really enjoy and that will help you better bond with your Pug.

CHAPTER 11.
Living With Other Dogs

Pugs love to be social, and that includes spending time with other dogs. Since they don't love being alone, it is usually best to have at least one other dog around to keep them company. This will reduce their anxiety too.

Pugs may like to be lazy or playful (instead of being trained); they are much happier being with you, doing what you want, over being alone. They don't have to be alpha, but they may have opinions on what you should be doing. If you aren't available, other dogs are a perfectly acceptable substitute. They do require socialization, and any other dog in your home will need some time to get accustomed to having a puppy or new dog in the house.

Introducing Your New Puppy

"One good tip is: if you have another dog it's important to bring them outside the house to meet the puppy when bringing it home for the first time. Then bring them into the house together."

Shelley Richfield
Richfield Pugs

HELPFUL TIP
Part of a Pack

Supervision is key when introducing your new puppy to the other four-legged members of your family. Prepare for the initial meeting by putting away your other dogs' toys to avoid any territorial behaviors. Providing separate food and water dishes for each animal is advised. Be prepared for possible growling and snapping by the older dogs. It is a normal part of bringing another dog into the already- established family unit.

Your dog (or dogs) should meet your puppy in a neutral location. This will stop your dog from feeling territorial, though there may be some jealousy with a puppy being close to you. The jealousy will likely be minimized since the focus is going to be on the dog meeting the puppy. This means that your dog is going to be more interested in the puppy than probably almost anything else. The important thing is that the meeting is at a place that won't

make your dog feel like the puppy is trespassing. No matter what breed of dog you have, the first meeting should always be introduced in a neutral place.

As your new family member and the rest of the canine pack start to get acquainted and feel comfortable with each other, you can head home. As they enter the home, they will have a bit more familiarity with each other, making your current dogs feel more comfortable with the new addition to the family. This sense of familiarity does not mean that they will be bonded, so there may be some tension, especially early on. This is why it is important to keep them separated when you aren't home. The puppy should be in the designated area, and it will be easier for your puppy to relax and start to get familiar with the new environment there. Since you set the special area up prior to your puppy's arrival, it will be much easier to start getting your puppy acclimated to his area.

Make sure that none of your other dog's stuff ends up in the puppy's area. This can be seen by your dog as a threat to his or her place in the pack and will generate unnecessary tension between your dog and the new puppy. The puppy will probably chew on anything and everything in the puppy's area, including things that belong to your other dog. At this stage, possessions don't mean anything to your little Pug. Your dog, on the other hand, will see this as a challenge, likely resulting in very negative behavior. This will be true when your puppy is out of the puppy area too. Make sure that all of your dog's stuff is out of the puppy's reach at all times. Before taking the puppy out of the designated area, make sure to do a bit of cleanup and store the other dog's toys in a safe place.

Photo Courtesy of
Maya Hofacker

Mealtime is another potential problem, so your puppy should be eating in a different location, at least in the beginning. Food tends to be the source of most dog fights and unnecessary tension. As your puppy gets older, you can start to feed your Pug with your other dogs, but keep them separated.

Your current dog probably isn't going to be happy about sharing you with the puppy either. Be prepared to make sure your dog knows you still care about him or her after the puppy arrives because your dog is going to be pretty uncertain with the new addition. Schedule one-on-one time with your dog, including longer walks, extra training, or general play. This will let your dog know that the puppy is not a replacement. You should start keeping a schedule with your dog so that you don't change the amount of time you spend together after the puppy arrives. It also means you will need to be just as firm and consistent with your puppy as you are with your dog. If you are more lenient with your puppy than with your dog, this will create tension between your dog and the puppy.

There are a number of benefits to having a dog in the home who already knows the rules. The biggest is that your dog will also start scolding your puppy for misbehavior. Since your dog isn't likely to be swayed by how cute the puppy is, your dog will have a much more objective approach to training. Of course, your dog cannot be the primary trainer, but it is nice to have someone helping reinforce the rules and showing the puppy how things are done. Having a dog to set an example helps the puppy better understand where he or she is in the pack while learning what behaviors are unacceptable. As long as your dog is gentle with the new member of the family, it is all right to let your well-behaved dog scold and reprimand your puppy—just make sure there isn't too much aggression or roughness to the behavior correction. Having your own canine babysitter also helps establish a better relationship between the canines.

Should your dog opt out of this role, that isn't a problem either. There is no need to force a role on your current dogs because their behavior will be enough to show the puppy how to behave. It is best to let your dog decide what kind of relationship to have with the puppy.

Companion Dog Mentality

Photo Courtesy of Ian Nosek

Pugs love to have people and dogs around. They are not great at being alone and can be destructive (even if unintentionally) when left alone. Having another dog in the home will help your Pug feel less anxious when there are no people around the home. They can become just as attached to other dogs as people because they are not a picky breed. Their main focus is on having fun and relaxing—no matter who is present. Being alone is both boring and anxiety inducing for Pugs.

The best way to keep your Pug happy is to make sure there is never any alone time. As your Pug ages, it is very likely that some alone time will be appreciated, but generally only on your Pug's terms. He will want to be able to escape for a bit, but will still want people and dogs around for when he is ready to play or relax.

Biting, Fighting, and Puppy Anger Management

One of the reasons that people do not want to start with a puppy is because of how challenging puppies can be. Pug are typically even-tempered and adorable, but as puppies, they are also bursting with energy and do not know the rules. This means that they are going to be much more boisterous and potentially a danger to themselves or others. Even a laidback puppy can instigate a fight when riled up, and that energy can really get on a dog's nerves (particularly older dogs). There will be times when even your Pug is not happy, and this may result in tantrums and lashing out at your dog. It isn't common, but that doesn't mean it won't happen.

An untrained Pug will take on the personality of the stereotypical small dog monster. To avoid this, you really have to start training your puppy early. Aggression isn't often a problem, but training can make sure that aggression isn't something your puppy adopts because there is no training to teach the puppy not to behave in that way. If you see your Pug starting to be aggressive (not just playing), immediately step in and let the puppy know that is not acceptable.

Raising Multiple Puppies at Once

Only brave puppy parents adopt more than one puppy at a time, and this is true even with dogs like the Pug. It is at least twice as much work, and you will have to split your attention between two or more puppies at the same time. If you want to raise more than one Pug puppy at once, you are in for a real challenge. They are going to want to please you and spend time with you, but they are also likely to feel something similar for each other. They will have the same energy level and desire to learn, which means that their misbehaviors can feed off each other. It will take a lot more energy and work to make sure they behave the way you want them to act.

Be prepared to lose your personal life, particularly your social life, if you have more than one puppy at a time. Taking care of those little puppies is going to be like two full-time jobs. It is necessary to put a lot of work into training your puppies so that your home isn't destroyed twice as fast.

First, you must spend time with them both, together and separately. This means spending twice as much time with the puppies, making sure they get along well, learn at an even pace, and still get to have designated time with you. Each puppy will have its own strengths and weaknesses, and you need to learn what those are for each one, as well as learning how well the puppies work together. If they both behave during alone time with you but tend to misbehave or fail to listen when they are together,

you will need to adjust your approach to make sure they both understand the rules. This is a real challenge, especially if they whine when you are playing with one of them and not the other (which is very likely with Pugs).

You can always have someone else play or train with one puppy while you do the same with the other, then switch puppies. This builds bonds while letting the puppies know that they both have to listen to you and your training partner. Both puppies will also be happily occupied, so they won't be whimpering or feeling lonely while you are playing with the other puppy.

There may be some fighting between the puppies, and this is likely to start when they are between three and six months of age. They don't tend to be as aggressive as other dogs, but it is still almost certain that there will be minor fights. This is fine as long as they are not too aggressive. It probably won't happen much because Pugs are less concerned with where they are in the hierarchy than with being with their people. As long as they understand the rules and abide by them, fighting should not be a significant problem with your puppies.

During training, you will need to minimize distractions, both for your puppy and yourself. This is why serious training should be done one-on-one more often than together. Puppies are always watching and learning, especially when you have a dog that is as enamored with you as Pugs tend to be. If you do not properly train them, it will be your fault when they become difficult adults who won't listen to you. Be consistent and focused during training to avoid the worst behavior problems.

CHAPTER 12.
Training Your Pug Puppy

Pugs are able to figure things out much faster than most small dogs, and even a large percentage of the canine realm. Despite a lot of energy and a desire to enjoy their time with you, training is probably going to be easier than with many other small dogs (though not as easy as with working dogs and really intelligent breeds). Pugs can be stubborn. However, with a firm and consistent approach, your Pug will learn to respect and listen to you.

Working with a smart, energetic puppy can be tiring. By making sure to follow through with a few actions, you will find that your Pug will pick up on the training much quicker. Keep in mind that training your puppy is a long-term commitment. Even if your Pug isn't rebellious, the puppy probably just wants to have fun. Your puppy won't want to anger you, but gentle begging and puppy eyes can be very effective, and Pugs will learn that, particularly if you give in during a training session.

Firm and Consistent

HELPFUL TIP
Who is the Boss?

Pugs are known for their stable temperament. These amiable extroverts want to please their owners and can be nearly painless to train. Secure your dog's respect early on in your relationship to achieve success. Keep in mind that pugs are prone to obesity, so be cautious when giving treats to reinforce positive behavior. Love, affection, and constructive attention go a long way toward training your puppy.

There are many times in life where you will feel something is close enough. This is never a good idea with intelligent dogs. They study their people and figure out ways to get what they want with as little work as possible. Wanting to please you will still drive a Pug, but if you are willing to give an inch, he will take it and see how much further you can be pushed. Exceptions and leniency are seen by your puppy as having some control over the situation, and that is not something you want him to learn when he is young. It just makes it that much harder to make him take you seriously later.

Keeping a consistent and firm approach during training will make life for easier for you and your puppy. Even if you are tired at the end of a long day at work, you have to enforce the rules. No matter how cute or friendly your puppy is being, you must make sure that all of the rules you have been teaching remain firmly in place. If you don't feel up to it, have a family member do the training. If you don't have anyone to help you, you can change up the training a bit to make it more enjoyable. It is fine to change things up if you are having a rough time, as long as you remain consistent. Interacting with your Pug can make for a much more enjoyable experience, and can even cheer you up. Consistency and firmness do not mean that you have to do the same thing all of the time. You just need to make sure that your puppy understands that you are in charge and there is no negotiating on that. This will keep your puppy on the right track to being a great companion instead of a little dictator.

Gain Respect Early

Being firm and consistent in your approach to training will start gaining you respect from your little canine early in your relationship. This is something you will need to keep building over time. Without respect, your Pug is going to think you don't mean what you say and will start to try to get its own way. As long as you are firm and consistent, respect should be a natural part of the bond. That does mean that you cannot multitask while you are training your puppy, or even just playing with your puppy. The Pug wants your full attention and will find a way to get it, even if it means breaking the rules to get your attention.

Positive reinforcement is the best way to gain respect, particularly if you use positive interaction. Playing and training your puppy every day helps build a healthy, positive relationship that will teach your puppy where he or she fits into the pack. Your puppy will learn that it is part of the family, but that you are the one in charge.

Operant Conditioning Basics

Operant conditioning is the scientific term for actions and consequences. What you have to do is provide your Pug puppy with the right consequences for each behavior.

The best way to use operant conditioning is through positive reinforcement, particularly since Pugs are so attached to people. This type of training is more effective with working dogs and dogs that have a long history with people because they want to please their people. They want to work with you and fulfill their tasks. Knowing that they are doing something right does a lot more to encourage their behavior than knowing when they do something wrong. With so much energy, they will be able to keep trying until they get it right.

There are two types of reinforcements for operant conditioning:

- Primary reinforcements
- Secondary reinforcements

You will use both during your Pug training.

Primary Reinforcements

A primary reinforcement gives your dog something that it needs to survive, like food or social interaction. Both of these can be effective for Pugs—they love spending time with you and may be happy to have treats. That is exactly what makes treats so effective during training.

Photo Courtesy of Shelley Richfield

Initially, you will rely on primary reinforcements since you do not have to teach your Pug to enjoy them. However, you have to keep a balance. Mealtime and playtime should never be denied to your puppy, no matter how poorly the puppy performs. These things are essential to living, and you will have to give them the essentials—that is not negotiable. It is things like treats and extra playtime that you will use to reinforce good behavior.

Err on the side of providing too much attention and affection over too many treats. Because of their small stature, Pug need to keep a well-balanced diet to be healthy. If you rely on treats instead of attention, you are setting yourself and your pup up for serious problems later.

Secondary Reinforcements

You used repetition to get good at your hobbies, sports, and other physical activities—this is secondary reinforcement. Without a doubt, Pavlov's experiment with dogs is the most recognizable example of secondary reinforcement. Using the bell, Pavlov taught the test dogs that when the bell rang, it meant it was time to eat. The dogs began to associate the ringing of a bell to mealtime. They were conditioned to associate something with a primary reinforcement. You can see this in your home when you use a can opener. If you have any cats or dogs, they probably come running as soon as the can opener starts going.

Secondary reinforcements work because your Pug will associate the trigger with something that is required. This makes your puppy more likely to do as you tell it to do. Dogs that are taught to sit using a treat only will automatically react by sitting down when you have a treat in your hand. They won't even wait for you to tell them to sit. They know that sitting means more food, so they automatically do it once you make that association. Of course, this is not proper training because they need to learn to sit when you say sit, and not when you have a treat. That is the real challenge.

Fortunately, it is relatively easy to train Pug puppies with the right trigger because they are both intelligent and eager to please. While they may enjoy food, you can show them that the trigger is the word, not the food. They will get it much faster than many other dog breeds.

You can also use toys and attention as a way of getting your Pug to do the right thing. If you have a regular schedule and you are willing to change it a little to give your puppy a little extra attention for doing something right, that will be just as effective as a treat because they love attention. You can take the pup on an extra walk, spend a little more time playing with a favorite toy, or take some time to cuddle with the puppy.

Sometimes punishment is required too, but you need to be very careful about how you do it. Trying to punish a Pug can be tricky, but denying your Pug attention can work very well. Simply put your puppy in a penned-off area where the Pug can see you but cannot interact with you. The little guy will whine and whimper to let you know that he or she wants out. Don't give in because this is the punishment. Just ignore your puppy to teach the lesson about proper behavior.

Punishments must happen right after the event. If your Pug chews something up and you don't find out for several hours, it is too late to punish the puppy. The same is true for rewards. To reinforce behavior, the reward or punishment must be almost immediate. When you praise or punish your puppy, make sure you keep eye contact. You can also take the puppy by the scruff of the neck to ensure that you keep eye contact. You won't need to do that when you are praising your pooch because he or she will automatically keep eye contact. Pugs can be absolutely driven by hearing your praise.

Why Food Is a Bad Reinforcement Tool

The small Pug stature means that food is not something you should use often as a reward. It does not take much for a Pug to gain too much weight. With affection and attention being such successful motivators, it is best to use them as much as possible instead of getting your Pug accustomed to treats for rewards. Use treats sparingly.

Photo Courtesy of Aimee Harten

Another reason to use treats sparingly is because you don't want your puppy to respond to you primarily when you have food. If your Pug associates training with treats, you may have a difficult time training your Pug to listen to you without them.

Treats can be used in the early stages when your puppy's metabolism is high and has not been conditioned to respond to secondary reinforcement. This will give you something to help your puppy learn to focus as you train the puppy to understand other incentives. It should not take too long before you can start transitioning away from treats as a reinforcement tool. Treats are also the best way of training certain types of behavior, such as rolling over. Your puppy will automatically follow the treat, making it easy to understand what you mean.

Treats are also best for the beginning commands (sit, stay, and leave it). Your dog does not understand words yet, and will quickly make the connection between what you are saying and why the treat is being offered. Leave it is very difficult to teach without treats because there is no incentive to drop something if your puppy really wants the object already in his or her mouth. Treats are something that will make the puppy drop whatever is in his mouth as the attention and desire focuses on food.

Small Steps to Success

The first few weeks, or maybe even the first couple of months, are a time with a very steep learning curve. Your puppy is not going to understand what you are doing in the beginning as you try to convince your little Pug to use the bathroom outside. The best way to train the puppy is to realize that you need to start slow—don't begin with expectations that your puppy will be house-trained in a week (that won't happen). Your puppy must learn the daily routine (which you will be doing at the same time). Once the schedule and environment are less exciting, your Pug will have an easier time focusing during training sessions.

Training should begin from day one. Even through your puppy is just getting to know the environment, you need to start putting some of the rules in place. As your puppy gets familiar with you and the environment, you can teach the Pug about its area and that the crate is for sleeping. Learning to go into the crate on command has some obvious benefits, particularly if you leave home every day. This is when you start using treats to train the puppy to go into the crate and do other basic activities.

Starting from day one does not mean trying to do everything—you must start small. Give treats for little things that your puppy might do anyway, like exploring the crate. Once your Pug starts to understand the reward system, training will start to get easier.

Why Trainers Aren't Always Necessary

Pugs really aren't the type of dog that requires trainers because they are more than happy to listen to their people. Even if you want to train your Pug to do more complicated tricks, you probably don't need a trainer, unless you are a complete novice with teaching puppies. Then the training is really more for you than for the puppy.

Pugs have been lapdogs for centuries, but unlike a lot of small dogs, they have enjoyed interacting with people and playing instead of just being lazy. They have energy and want to put it to good use. Watching them bounce around can be very therapeutic at the end of the day, which can make it as much of a way for you to unwind as it is a way for your puppy to learn.

If you have older dogs, they can be a great way of keeping your Pug in check when you are gone—after your Pug has been in the home for a couple of months. You will need to use the crate in the beginning, but with time, your older dog can be a great role model for how to while away the day in your absence. In the beginning, your absence should be very short, like going to get the mail. Then you can progress to slightly longer activities that take you out of the house for half an hour or so. With an older dog in charge, this can help your Pug be more comfortable when you aren't around the home.

If you don't have much time once the basics are done, you should consider getting a trainer to make sure your puppy doesn't forget the basics (although you are not off the hook). Since your Pug will more likely react quicker to your training though, it is well worth making sure you always have time for your puppy because no trainer is going to be as influential as you are—your puppy loves you, and if you want those tricks to stick, you will have to participate and keep up the training.

CHAPTER 13.
Basic Commands

Not all Pugs are good at learning tricks, but if you start when your Pug is a puppy, you are guaranteed to get at least the basics ingrained into their minds. It also significantly increases the odds that your Pug will be able to learn more advanced tricks later. By establishing the training relationship, your Pug will learn to listen and understand what will result in those delicious treats.

Why Size and Personality Make Them Ideal Companions

Training is something that is a lot of fun with a Pug. They are incredibly intelligent, and training them makes them even more fun to spend time with. When properly trained, they can be one of the best companions because they can travel with you anywhere you go. If a Pug is well trained, the people around you will also enjoy having the dog around, too, because Pugs are famous for their fun and energy. They tend to love everyone and want to play. Since they can go with you virtually anywhere, training will quickly pay off as you and your best friend share some of the most memorable lessons. If your Pug is not trained, it will be much harder to take your canine places as your Pug will be wary of strangers and may bark far more than is comfortable for anyone around them.

Picking the Right Reward

One of the most interesting aspects of having a Pug is determining the right reward. You want to keep the treats to a minimum, but that should be fine with a Pug since there are so many other things that can motivate them. Treats may be a good starting point, but you will need to quickly switch to something that is a secondary reinforcer. Praise, additional playtime, and extra petting are all fantastic rewards for Pug pets since they care about how you feel and your reaction to them. Plopping down to watch a movie and letting the puppy sit with you will be a great reward after an intense training session. Not only did your puppy learn, but you both now get to relax and enjoy just chilling together.

Photo Courtesy of
Kirsten O'Steen Faulkner

If you begin to gain the respect of your Pug, that can be used to help train your dog. At the end of each session, give your puppy extra attention or a nice walk to demonstrate how pleased you are with the progress that has been made.

Successful Training

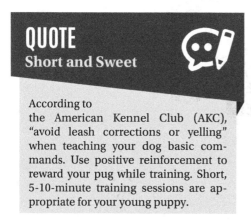

QUOTE

Short and Sweet

According to the American Kennel Club (AKC), "avoid leash corrections or yelling" when teaching your dog basic commands. Use positive reinforcement to reward your pug while training. Short, 5-10-minute training sessions are appropriate for your young puppy.

Training is about learning the commands. If your Pug learns to respond only to the rewards (such as the dog that sits as soon as you have a treat in your hand), the training was not successful.

Gaining the respect of your dog is generally the key in being a successful trainer, but with a Pug, it also means dedicated attention—you have all of the puppy's attention during a training session. As you and your Pug work together, your dog will come to respect you (so long as you remain consistent and firm). Do not expect respect in the early days of training because your puppy does not have the understanding or relationship required to be able to understand. Fortunately, his intelligence will start to show early on, making it easy to see when he is starting to respond to you instead of just the reward. This is the time when you can start switching to rewards that are fun instead of those that center around treats and food.

Even in the beginning, you need to make handling and petting a part of the reward. Although your dog does not quite understand it for what it is, your Pug will begin to understand that treats and petting are both types of rewards. This will make it easier to switch from treats to a more attention-based reward system. Associating handling and petting as being enjoyable will also encourage your puppy to look at playtime as a great reward. No matter how much he loves to eat, being entertained and playing with you will be a welcome reward since it means the puppy is not alone or bored.

Basic Commands

For the Pug, there are five basic commands that you must teach, and ones that you will probably want to start training your puppy to understand. These commands are the basis for a happy and enjoyable relationship as your Pug learns how to behave. By the time your puppy learns the five commands, the purpose of training will be clear to your Pug. That will make it much easier to train him on the more complex concepts.

You should train the puppy in the order of the list as well. Sit is a basic command, and something all dogs, as well as your Pug, already do. Teaching leave it and how to bark less are both difficult and fight the instincts and desires of your Pug pooch. They are going to take longer to learn than the other commands, so you want to have the necessary tools already in place to increase your odds of success.

Here are some basic guidelines to follow during training.

- Everyone in the home should be a part of the Pug training because the Pug needs to learn to listen to everyone in the household, and not just one or two people.

- To get started, select an area where you and your puppy have no distractions, including noise. Leave your phone and other devices out of range so that you keep your attention on the puppy.

- Stay happy and excited about the training. Your puppy will pick up on your enthusiasm and will focus better because of it.
- Start to teach sit when your puppy is around eight weeks old.
- Be consistent and firm as you teach.
- Bring a special treat to the first few training sessions, such as chicken or cheese.

Once you are prepared, you can get started working and bonding with your cute little Pug.

Sit

Once you settle into your quiet training location with the special treat, begin the training. It is relatively easy to train your dog to obey this command. Wait until your puppy starts to sit down and say sit as he or she sits. If your puppy finishes sitting down, start to give praise for it. Naturally, this will make your puppy incredibly excited and wiggly, so it may take a bit of time before he or she will want to sit again. When the time comes and the puppy starts to sit again, repeat the process.

It is going to take more than a couple of sessions for the puppy to fully connect your words with the actions. In fact, it could take a little over a week for your puppy to get it. Pugs are intelligent, but at this age, there is still so much to learn that the puppy will have a hard time focusing. Commands are something completely new to your little companion. However, once your puppy understands your intention and masters sit, the other commands will likely be a little bit easier to teach.

Once your puppy has demonstrated mastery over sit, it is time to start teaching down.

Down

Repeat the same process to teach this command as you did for sit. Wait until the puppy starts to lie down, then say the word. If the Pug finishes the action, offer your chosen reward.

It will probably take a little less time to teach this command after you start training it.

Wait until your puppy has mastered down before moving on to stay.

Stay

This command is going to be more difficult since it isn't something that your puppy does naturally. Be prepared for it to take a bit longer to train on this one. It is also important that your dog has mastered and will consistently sit and lie down on command before you start to teach stay.

Choose which of these two commands you want to use to get started, and then you will need to be consistent. Once your dog understands stay for either sit or down, you can train with the second command. Just make sure the first position is mastered before trying the second.

Tell your puppy to either sit or stay. As you do this, place your hand in front of the puppy's face. Wait until the puppy stops trying to lick your hand before you begin again.

When the puppy settles down, take a step away from the Pug. If your puppy is not moving, say stay and give the puppy the treat and some praise for staying.

Giving the reward to your puppy indicates that the command is over, but you also need to indicate that the command is complete. The puppy has to learn to stay until you say it is okay to leave the spot. Once you give the okay to move, do not give treats. Come should not be used as the okay word as it is a command used for something else.

Repeat these steps, taking more steps further from the puppy after a successful command.

Once your puppy understands stay when you move away, start training to stay even if you are not moving. Extend the amount of time required for the puppy to stay in one spot so that he or she understands that stay ends with the okay command.

When you feel that your puppy has stay mastered, start to train the puppy to come.

Come

This is the last in the series of commands since you cannot teach this one until the puppy has learned the previous commands. The other two commands do not require the puppy to know other commands to get started (it is just easier to train if the puppy already has an understanding of what commands are and how the puppy is expected to react to them).

Before you start, decide if you want to use come or come here for the command. You will need to be consistent in the words you use, so make sure you plan it so that you will intentionally use the right command every time.

Leash the puppy.

Tell the puppy to stay. Move away from the puppy.

Say the command you will use for come and give a gentle tug on the leash toward you. As long as you did not use the term to indicate that the stay command was done, your puppy will begin to understand the purpose of your new command. If you used the term to indicate the end of stay, it will confuse your puppy because the Pug will associate the command with being able to move freely.

Repeat these steps, building a larger distance between you and the puppy. Once the puppy seems to get it, remove the leash and start at a close distance. If your puppy does not seem to understand the command, give some visual clues about what you want. For example, you can pat your leg or snap your fingers. As soon as your puppy comes running over to you, offer a reward.

Leave It

This is going to be one of the most difficult commands you will teach your puppy because it goes against both your puppy's instincts and interests. Your puppy wants to keep whatever he or she has, so you are going to have to offer something better. It is essential to teach it early though, as your Pug is going to be very destructive in the early days. You want to get the trigger in place to convince the puppy to drop things.

You may need to start teaching this command outside of the training arena as it has a different starting point.

Start when you have time to dedicate yourself to the lesson. You have to wait until the puppy has something in his or her mouth to drop. Toys are usually best. Offer the puppy a special treat. As the Pug drops the toy, say leave it, and hand over the treat.

This is going to be one of those rare times when you must use a treat because your puppy needs something better to convince him or her to drop the toy. For now, your puppy needs that incentive, something more tempting than what he or she already has, before your puppy can learn the command.

This will be one of the two commands that will take the longest to teach (quiet being the other). Be prepared to be patient with your pup. Once your puppy gets it, start to teach leave it with food. This is incredibly important to do because it could save your pooch's life. He is likely to lunge at things that look like food when you are out for a walk, and being so low to the ground, he is probably going to see a lot of food-like things long before you do. This command gets him to drop whatever he is munching on before ingesting it.

Quiet

In the beginning, you can also use treats sparingly to reinforce qui-et. If your puppy is barking for no apparent reason, tell the puppy to be quiet and place a treat nearby. It is almost guaranteed that the dog will fall silent to sniff the treat, in which case, say good dog or good quiet. It will not take too long for your puppy to understand that quiet means no barking. However, it may take a while for your puppy to learn to fight the urge to bark. Be patient with your puppy because it is difficult to stop do-ing something that you do naturally. How long did it take you to learn to get up early in the morning or to go to bed at a certain time? It is similar for a Pug to learn not to bark.

Where to Go From Here

These are all the commands that you are likely to need with your Pug. However, if you want your Pug to do tricks, you can pretty much go anywhere from here. These commands are the foundation of training, and the Pug is capable of learning so much more. Just make sure that the tricks that you teach your Pug are not too stressful for your puppy. As your puppy ages, you can start teaching tricks that highlight your pup-py's agility. Fetch and other interactive tricks will be ideal because your Pug will want to do them.

CHAPTER 14.
Nutrition

Nutrition is just as important for your Pug as it is for you. Most people want to take good care of their dogs. However, it is just as easy to fall into the habit of offering food that is decidedly unhealthy for canines. From letting them have scraps from your plate to providing far too many treats, many pets end up getting far too many calories for their activity levels. As your dog ages, this could become a serious issue for the canine's health. For Pugs, you even have to be careful about the kind of dog food you purchase. Ensuring your Pug gets the right nutritional balance is critical for a long, happy life.

Why a Healthy Diet is Important

Though they have a considerable amount of energy, Pugs are a very small breed. Overfeeding them is incredibly easy because they do not need a whole lot of food before they reach their caloric needs for the day. Many of the tricks and activities that they do can expend a good bit of energy, but that does not mean that they need a lot of food. If you have a very

busy schedule, it will be entirely too easy to have substantial lapses in activity levels while you are home. Your Pug is still going to expect the same amount of food, regardless of activity level. This means he is likely to start putting on weight, which will be detrimental to his health.

HELPFUL TIP
Pug Lifestyle

Let's be honest.
Your pug would be content to sleep on the sofa and only move when the dinner bell rings. It is up to you to watch his diet and keep his caloric intake within healthy limits. Seek advice from your veterinarian on what and how much to feed your pet to promote lifelong wellness. Exercise is very important and is good for both you and your pet.

You need to not only be careful of how much you feed your Pug during mealtime, but of how many treats you offer over the course of the day. All food needs to be considered when you consider both nutritional and caloric intake. With those tiny little bodies, you need to be aware of roughly how many calories your dog eats a day. If you notice that your dog is putting on weight, you will be able to adjust how much food the Pug eats a day, or change the food to something with more nutritional value.

Breeders also recommend that you avoid food made of grains. Grains can make them gain weight faster. If you have the time, it is best to make your dog's meals—or at the least provide real food mixed with dog food.

Commercial Food

Though it is convenient, commercial dog food is a very flawed product. There is nothing natural about those little bits of food you are feeding your dog, and ultimately, it is far less healthy than making your dog's meals. However, for most people, it is the option that will be chosen because preparing every meal is an incredibly lengthy process. For some, there simply isn't adequate time in the day to make every meal.

If you are one of the majority of puppy parents, make sure that you are buying the best that you can. Take the time to research each of your options, particularly the nutritional value of the food. Always account for your dog's small stature, energy levels, and age. Your puppy may not need puppy food as long as other breeds (or even other Pugs), and dog food for seniors may not be the best option for your senior Pug. To provide more nutrition, you can mix some home-cooked food into the processed food. This can help supplement any nutrients, as well as being a healthy addition to an otherwise entirely processed meal. The addition of a little bit of home-cooked food with each meal will make your Pug excited to eat.

Preparing Your Food Naturally at Home

If you want to provide the healthiest meals possible, you should plan to spend an extra five to ten minutes in the kitchen per meal you prepare for your Pug. If you regularly make your own food (from scratch, not with a microwave or boxed meal), it really doesn't take that much more time to provide an equally healthy meal for your little companion.

Keeping in mind the foods that your Pug absolutely should not eat, you can mix some of the food you make for yourself in your Pug's meal. Just make sure to add a bit more of what your Pug needs to the puppy food bowl. Although you and your Pug have distinctly different dietary needs, you can tailor your foods to include nutrients that your dog needs. It won't really take that much longer to tailor a meal for you and a slightly different version for your dog. Read through Chapter 5 to make sure that you never give your Pug food that could be harmful or deadly.

Do not feed your Pug from your plate. Split the food, placing your dog's meal into a bowl so that your canine understands that your food is just for you. The best home-cooked meals should be planned in advance so that your Pug is getting the right nutritional balance.

Typically, 50 percent of your dog's food should be animal protein (fish, poultry, and organ meats). About 25 percent should be full of complex carbohydrates. The remaining 25 percent should be from fruits and vegetables, particularly foods like pumpkin, apples, bananas, and green beans. These provide additional flavor that your Pug will likely love while making the little pup feel full faster so that overeating is reduced.

Puppy Food vs. People Food

It is true that puppies need more calories than adults, and with their small size, Pug puppies do not need nearly as much as you may think they do to meet caloric needs for their energy levels. If you are bringing a Pug puppy into your home and know that you aren't going to have the time to cook, you should get food designed for puppies. This will ensure that your puppy gets the necessary calories for growth. Do not feed the puppy people food under the belief that you can switch to dog food later—because that is going to be virtually impossible later. Once your Pug becomes an adult, it is nearly impossible to convince your canine that those unappe-

Photo Courtesy of Amanda Michael

tizing pellets are food, particularly when your dog knows what the food on your plate tastes like. Do not set a precedent that will create significant problems for yourself later. If you feed your Pug puppy food, you are going to have to keep making food for your dog once the puppy stage is a memory.

It is best to make your puppy's food if you can. There really isn't going to be that much of a difference in the amount of food between the puppy and adult stages. Their little bodies have special needs, and the first few months are critical. If you can make your puppy's meals (and know that you can keep it up when your Pug is an adult), this will be a lot healthier for your dog.

If you find that you have to start buying commercial food, you will need to start slowly mixing it into your adult dog's meal. Do not be surprised if you find the pellets are uneaten for a while. It will be a difficult process convincing your dog that this is food, but if you mix it with other things (and know that you are always going to need to mix at least a little real food in with the commercial food), your dog will be more likely to start eating it since it will smell like real food.

Dieting, Exercise, and Obesity

"Pugs can get overweight quickly because of their obsession with food and having such a short stubby figure. You have to be mindful early on and check with your vet for the appropriate diet for your growing Pug."

Laela Cottone
Thunderstorms Pug Pals

Photo Courtesy of Aimee Harten

Your Pug is not going to diet the way you may choose to diet. This means you have to keep a regular eating schedule for your dog—his day is going to be based largely on the times of the day that are designated for eating. If treats and snacks are something you establish as normal early on, your dog is going to believe that is also a part of the routine and will expect it. Obviously, this can be a terrible habit to establish with your Pug, especially if it is food that you are sharing because you are snacking and feel guilty. You will need to make sure to be active after snacking so that your Pug doesn't get too many calories. An extra round of play or another walk can go a long way to helping keep your Pug at a healthy weight.

There needs to be a healthy balance of diet and exercise to keep your Pug from becoming overweight, certainly to avoid your dog getting obese. Exercise is an absolute must. While you are helping your Pug develop healthy eating and exercise habits, you are probably helping yourself. Becoming more aware of your dog's diet and exercise levels will probably make you more aware of your own. Obesity is something that you will need to actively avoid with a small dog. Get used to exercising and playing as a reward system.

Warning About Overfeeding and the Right Caloric Requirement

You have to be careful of your Pug's weight, so you need to get used to monitoring it, particularly once your dog is an adult. Those snacks you share are not healthy, and your dog will pick up weight a lot faster than you will eating the same foods with less exercise. This is not really a reward for your Pug—it's a hazard. Keep your dog on a diet that is healthy instead of indulging the little cutie. This will keep you both a lot happier in the long run.

Weighing your Pug will be incredibly helpful to ensuring that the pooch is staying at a healthy weight. Because they are really toy-sized, you can use your own scales to weigh them. Gently pick up your canine and step on the scale. Subtract your weight from the total, and that is how much your Pug weighs. Be honest about your weight. That does mean weighing yourself just before weighing your Pug and being accurate with the number. Counting calories is incredibly time-consuming, but you should also know roughly how many calories your Pug eats in a day because it really does not take much to meet the needs of such a small dog.

CHAPTER 15.
Grooming – Productive Bonding

Pugs have short hair that is fairly coarse. However, with the constant petting and attention, it will feel reasonably soft. The problem comes when the dog sheds—and that is pretty much always. Since he has such a small body, you will be shocked by just how much your Pug will shed. While you won't be able to stop the shedding, there is a lot you can do to minimize how much fur you have rolling around your home. Mostly, you are going to need to brush your dog—this is not a breed that requires special attention to the coat. Apart from frequent brushing, you aren't going to need to worry about getting the dog's hair styled or washed as often as small dogs with long hair require.

Managing Your Pug's Coat

Weekly, or even daily brushing, is the perfect way to bond with your puppy and to keep the relationship strong well into your Pug's golden years. The regular attention will be something that your dog will look forward to as a part of the routine. It will also be a nice way to relieve stress as petting a dog is an easy way to help you calm down. Since Pugs are fairly small, it isn't going to be the chore that managing a large dog will be. This makes it a quick and easy task that everyone can enjoy.

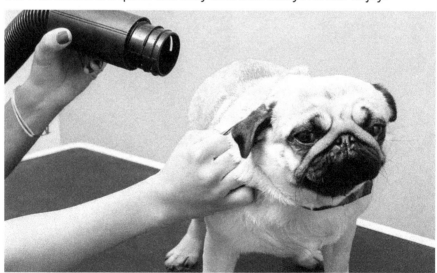

Puppy

As you can probably guess, brushing a puppy is going to take you more time. There will be a lot of wiggling and attempts at play. Trying to tell your puppy that the brush is not a toy clearly isn't going to work, so be prepared to be patient during each brushing session. On the other hand, they are so adorable, you probably won't mind that it takes a bit longer.

You can plan to brush your puppy after vigorous exercise so that your Pug has far less energy to fight or play. Be careful that you don't encourage rambunctious behavior during brushing because this will become part of the routine, and your Pug will think that the brush is meant for playtime, and it is going to be difficult to convince him that it isn't true the longer it happens. Maybe you won't mind in the beginning, but there will be times when you just want to finish brushing your dog quickly, and that is why you need to make sure your puppy doesn't think it is time to play.

As you get accustomed to brushing your puppy, get accustomed to checking his skin. Look for rashes, sores, or infections. You should also check his ears and mouth while you are grooming him. Keep doing these activities even after your Pug is an adult. Since Pugs have such small bodies, it won't be that time- consuming, and it will help you to spot potential issues as early as possible.

Adulthood

"A good brushing once a week will help with shedding. We use Alaskan Salmon Oil for on our Pugs, it gives then awesome fur."

LaDonna Weaver
Hugapug Kennels

Tangles are not something you have to worry about with Pugs, but you do need to be careful of their skin. Brushing probably won't take too long, and you won't mind making it nearly a daily activity.

Baths should be a regular part of the schedule too, although it will vary based on the time of year. Another thing you need to clean regularly is the wrinkles on the face. These can trap dirt, making them potentially dangerous little areas that can become infected. This is a really quick activity, but you do need to be careful. Use a lightly damp cloth so that you don't make the folds of the wrinkles wet. Of course, you may not think of your Pug as having a face, but it is important to keep the folds clean.

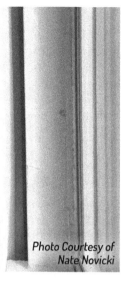

Photo Courtesy of Nate Novicki

Trimming the Nails

"Nails should be clipped or Dremeled once a month or more often with young pups. They are known for their extreme dislike of nail clipping! We have found they are much better for us if we use a Dremel."

Joan Yerkie
Snugglepugs

HELPFUL TIP
Low-maintenance Grooming

When it comes to grooming needs, your pug companion is considered a low-maintenance dog. Brushing your pet's coat weekly will help with the natural shedding of his coat. It is important to take your pug for professional nail trimming at least once a month. Overly long nails can lead to discomfort and eventual problems for your family pet.

Because Pugs have small paws, you have to be very careful about trimming the nails. If you feel at all uncomfortable, you might want to have a professional trim your Pug's nails. You can always study how it is done and learn how to do it yourself over time. While he is still a puppy though, your Pug may be a little too enthusiastic for you to do the cutting.

The puppy's nails should be cut about once a week

since your Pug will probably be on concrete and asphalt less often than a larger dog. Without these hard surfaces to help keep the nails filed, regular grooming will be required to keep the nails from being too long.

Once your dog is an adult, check the nails monthly. As you will be walking him more often on sidewalks or other kinds of surfaces that will help keep his nails shorter, grooming can be done less frequently. It is possible that you won't need to trim them for months at a time if your Pug walks on concrete or asphalt enough to keep his nails short. However, if you don't walk as much on these surfaces in the winter, you will need to increase how often you trim the nails.

Brushing Their Teeth

A Pug's teeth should be brushed at least once a week (twice or three times is recommended). Considering the fact that your Pug will be all over you, you will have a pretty good idea when to brush his teeth—if you can't stand the smell emanating from your dog's mouth, stop what you are doing and brush those teeth. Regular brushing keeps the dog's teeth clean and healthy. If you notice that plaque and tartar are building up quickly, or that your dog's breath is smelling foul faster, you can increase how often you conduct the brushing ritual.

Cleaning Their Eyes

You will need to take extra care of your Pug's eyes. They frequently tear up, and because they bulge out, they are prone to getting dirt in them. As you clean the wrinkles, you can take the time to keep the eyes clean. Wiping your pup's eyes daily with a damp cloth will help keep the staining to a minimum, as well as keeping dirt from accumulating around the eyes. Do not apply pressure. Gently wiping around the eyes should be adequate.

Photo Courtesy of Megan Schreck-Preston

CHAPTER 16.
Health Issues

Pugs make exceptionally fantastic companions, in large part due to their small stature and enthusiastic personalities. As long as you are careful and take good care of your little buddy, you will have well over a decade to enjoy your exuberant little companion. With such high excitement levels and a desire to keep playing, your Pug may not let you know if something hurts. While it is one reason to make sure no one plays too rough with your Pug, it also means that he may not let you know if they have another type of problem—fleas or ticks.

In addition to making sure that your canine doesn't get too excited, there are some basic preventative measures you should take to make sure your puppy stays healthy. Many of the treatments and concerns are universal across the entire canine world, which means there is a good chance you already know that you need to take care of your small dog. You can consider this chapter as more of a reminder or checklist of things you probably already know you need to be aware of. Treating and keeping your puppy free of parasites should be something that you add to your budget once he is old enough for the treatments.

Fleas and Ticks

Since Pugs don't require much outdoor time, they are at a lower risk of getting ticks. Fleas are something that you will need to watch for since they live in yards too. Your little Pug is going to be outside some of the time, which means you still have to monitor him. If your Pug loves roaming through high grass, you cannot allow any lapse in treatment, even in winter.

With each bath that you give your Pug, you should make time to check for ticks and fleas as part of the cleaning process. Comb through the fur and check the skin for irritation and parasites. This will help keep your puppy healthier and feeling much better. Since you will be doing this often, you should be able to know when a bump is a problem. Since your dog will be very happy to spend time with you, it shouldn't take as long as you think—it isn't as though you will have to spend a lot of time struggling to get your Pug to sit still for a tick check.

Fleas will be more problematic because they are far more mobile. The best way to look for fleas is to make it a regular part of your brushing sessions. You can also look for behavioral indicators, such as incessant scratching and licking. With the regular checks on your pup's skin when brushing his or her hair, you will be able to check the spots where your dog is scratching to see if the skin is irritated or if it is the work of a flea. Given the small stature of your companion, fleas will have no trouble jumping on your Pug from the grass or other vegetation. This means you will need to use flea preventative products on a regular basis. You won't be able to do this with puppies under a certain age, but once they mature, you can start adding treatment to the budget and schedule.

If you want to use natural products instead of the chemical-filled products, set aside a few hours to research the alternatives and find out what works best for your Pug. Do not increase the number of baths because their skin is sensitive and should not be washed too often, so increasing the frequency of baths should not be part of the solution. Do verify that any natural product purchases work before you buy them.

Remedies should be applied monthly. Establishing a regular schedule and adding it to the calendar will help you remember to treat your dog on schedule.

Worms and Parasites

Although worms and other types of parasites are a less common problem than fleas and ticks, they can be far more dangerous. There are a number of types of worms that you should be aware of:

- Heartworms
- Hookworms
- Roundworms
- Tapeworms
- Whipworms

One of the primary problems is that there isn't an easy to recognize set of symptoms to help identify when your dog has a problem with worms. However, you can keep an eye out for these symptoms, and if your dog shows them, you should schedule a visit to the vet.

Photo Courtesy of Stephanie Makar

- If your Pug is unexpectedly lethargic for at least a few days
- Patches of fur begin to fall out (this will be noticeable if you brush your Pug regularly) or if you notice patchy spaces in your dog's coat
- If your dog's stomach becomes distended (expands), set up an appointment immediately to have him or her checked. Your dog's stomach will look like a potbelly.
- Your Pug begins coughing, vomiting, has diarrhea, or has a loss in appetite.

These symptoms should be more obvious in a Pug because they tend to be active or with you all of the time. If you aren't sure, it is best to get to the vet as soon as possible to check.

If your dog has hookworms or roundworms, you will also need to visit a doctor to get checked. These worms can be spread to you from your dog through skin contact. If your dog has them, you are at risk of contracting them. Being treated at the same time can help stop the vicious cycle of continually switching which of you has worms.

Heartworms are a significant threat to your dog's health as they can be deadly. You should be actively treating your dog to ensure that this parasite does not have a home in your dog. There are medications that can ensure your Pug does not get or have heartworms.

Benefits of Veterinarians

Your dog should have regular visits to your vet, just like you have regular checkups for yourself. From regular shots to healthy checkups, vets will make sure that your Pug stays healthy. With a number of potential issues, you want to make sure that your Pug doesn't have any of the many possible problems.

Since Pugs are such eager companions, it is going to be obvious when they aren't acting normal. Annual visits to the vet will ensure there isn't a problem that is slowly draining the energy or health from your dog.

Health checkups also make sure that your Pug is aging well.

HELPFUL TIP
Choosing a Veterinarian

What should you look for when searching for a vet for your pug? The American Animal Hospital Association (AAHA) has a few suggestions. Visit the AAHA website (aahanet.org) for their list of accredited vets and animal hospitals in your area. Look around the veterinary hospital when you visit. Is it clean, hygienic, and organized? How many vets are on staff at the hospital? Do they have licensed veterinary technicians working at the facility? You will want a veterinarian who is willing to answer your questions and communicate effectively in order to create a comfortable working relationship with you and your pet.

If there are any early symptoms of something potentially wrong with your dog over the years (such as arthritis), you will be able to start making adjustments. The vet can help you come up with ways to manage pain and problems that come with the aging process. Your vet will be able to recommend adjustments to the schedule to accommodate your canine's aging body and diminishing abilities. This will ensure that you can keep having fun together without hurting your dog. These changes are well worth it in the end because your dog will able to keep enjoying time with you without suffering additional pain.

Photo Courtesy of Sydney Heinle

Holistic Alternatives

Wanting to keep a dog from a lot of exposure to chemical treatments makes sense, and there are many good reasons why people are moving to more holistic methods. However, doing this does require a lot more research and monitoring to ensure that the methods are working—and more importantly, which do not harm your dog. Unverified holistic medicines can be a waste of money, or worse, they can even be harmful to your pet. Other methods have often been used for far longer, so there is more data to ensure that they aren't doing more harm than good. However, natural methods that work are always preferable to any chemical solution.

If you decide to go with holistic medication, talk with your vet about your options. You can also seek out Pug experts to see what they recommend before you start using any methods you are interested in trying. Read what scientists have said about the medicine. There is a chance that the products you buy from a store are actually better than some holistic medications.

Make sure you are thorough in your research and that you do not take any unnecessary risks with the health of your Pug.

Vaccinating Your Pug

Vaccination schedules are almost universal for all dog breeds, including Pugs. Use the following to ensure that your Pug receives the shots needed on time.

- The first shots are required at between six and eight weeks following the birth of your Pug. You should find out from the breeder if these shots have been taken care of and get the records of the shots:
  - Corona virus
  - Distemper
  - Hepatitis
  - Leptospirosis
  - Parainfluenza
  - Parvo
- These same shots are required again at between 10 and 12 weeks of age.
- These same shots are required again at between 14 and 15 weeks old, as well as his or her first rabies shot.
- Your dog will need to get these shots annually after that. Your Pug will also need annual rabies shots afterwards.

Once you start the shots, you need to see them through to the end. Make sure to get the schedule for upkeep on these shots. Then you will need to maintain these shots over the years, particular shots like rabies.

CHAPTER 17.
Health Concerns

Having a purebred dog means that your canine has some known health issues that you will need to monitor for as he or she ages—and this is particularly true for a breed as old as the Pug. Knowing what the potential problems are so that you can watch for them can help you know what to do and when to talk to your vet. The sooner you start to counter any potential problems, the longer your Pug is likely to live and the healthier he or she is likely to be. This means more time enjoying each other's company. If you notice any of the symptoms listed in the earlier chapters, make sure to schedule an appointment with your vet to have your dog checked.

Photo Courtesy of Samantha Gerson

Adopting a puppy can give you the span of a dog's entire life to ensure your dog is as healthy as possible. The breeder should be able to provide health records in addition to any shot records and required tests. All of the details on the genetic and common ailments of Pug are in Chapter 4. Making sure that the parents are healthy increases the likelihood that your puppy will remain healthy over his or her entire life. However, there is still a chance that your dog will have one of these documented problems even if the parents don't, so you will still need to keep an eye on your little friend.

A Dog With a Lot of Possible Health Concerns

Some breeders will say that Pugs are a healthy breed. Others say that they aren't. This kind of inconsistency shows just how much of a variable genetics is.

There are two primary concerns that require your attention—your dog's face and compact little body.

Face

"Pugs have a Brachycephalic face structure. They have a short nose passage, which can cause the 'bulging eye' look. This is one reason they are not an extremely active breed. The short nose can make it hard for them in extreme heat, making cooling off their body difficult. It also makes it harder for the eye to drain properly, which is why they have more eye staining then some breeds."

Susan Bizier
Rainbow Pugs

The Pug's face is very distinctive. From the bulging eyes to the jutting teeth to the many wrinkles, the look of the Pug is entirely unique. As you fall in love with the way your little Pug's tongue curls up during the long panting bouts, you will need to keep in mind that it comes with a cost.

Because they have noses that are flat, Pugs can have trouble breathing. You have to be very careful to make sure your Pug never gets too hot. Heat is detrimental to Pugs since they cannot cool down as easily as other dogs.

The wrinkles are adorable, but also problematic. As covered in Chapter 15, grooming includes keeping the wrinkles clean.

All of these potential problems are because of breeding. Keep these in mind when playing with your Pug and making plans.

Body

The Pug's body looks incredibly sturdy, which tends to make people feel they can be rougher with the Pug. It's not true. Playing with Pugs is encouraged, but you always need to make sure that playtime does not include roughhousing. They can have problems with their hindquarters, so you need to be very mindful of arthritis and other problems as your Pug ages.

Typical Purebred Health Issues

Pugs are somewhat unpredictable when it comes to health issues. There is a rather long list of potential problems, but most Pugs tend to be healthy. This means that there is low risk, but that doesn't mean no risk. Keep a careful eye on your Pug over the years so that you are more likely to notice any potential issues.

Where You Can Go Wrong

In addition to genetic problems, there are things that you can do that could damage your dog's health. These are related to the dog's diet and exercise levels. If you follow the recommendations in Chapter 16, your dog will remain healthy longer.

Importance of Breeder to Ensuring Health In Your Pug

HELPFUL TIP
Specific Health Concerns

Pugs, like most breeds, have specific health concerns. They are prone to eye problems such as corneal ulcers and dry eyes. Breathing problems may occur especially in very warm weather or high humidity. Your vet should do a thorough hip evaluation and check for patella issues. Do not hesitate to ask the breeder about familial health issues in their dogs before investing your money and heart in a puppy.

Being aware of the health of the parents and the diseases that are known to be a problem for them or their parents will help you know what to monitor for in your Pug.

Any breeder that doesn't provide a health guarantee for a breed as established as the Pug is not a breeder you should consider. Avoid all of these breeders—they are interested in the money, and the dog's health is of little to no concern. If a breeder says that a puppy or litter has to be kept in an isolated location for health reasons, do not work with that breeder.

Ask the breeder to talk about the history of the parents, the kinds of health problems that have been in the dog's family, and if the breeder has had problems with any particular illness in the past. If the breeder gives you only short or vague answers, this is a sign that the breeder has dogs that are more likely to have issues later.

Common Diseases and Conditions

Pugs have problems with specific parts of their bodies a lot more often than most breeds. The following are the areas where you need to monitor your Pug:

1. *Nose and Breathing*

a. Brachycephalic Syndrome

This translates to "short-headed condition," and is a respiratory disorder. Dogs exhibit an enlarged soft palate, shrunken nostrils, small windpipe, or caved in voice box. Consider checking your dog if you observe labored or loud breathing or difficulty swallowing. Medication, oxygen therapy, weight loss, and surgery can help your dog live a better life.

b. Trachea Issues – Collapsing and Hypoplastic

This is determined by coughing, gagging, fast breathing, blue gums, or fainting. A collapsing trachea has no distinct cure, so maintaining a smoke free environment, managed diet, and light exercise are the best options. The less dangerous Hypoplastic trachea has similar symptoms, but is atypical cartilage growth around the windpipe, often accompanying heart defects.

c. Elongated Soft Palate (ESP)

This is common in tiny nosed dogs from birth. A dog's soft palate is similar to a human's uvula, and with ESP, this blocks the airways. Unique symptoms are vomiting, heat stroke, and snorting along with breathing problems and coughing. It is important to get necessary surgeries to prevent heart problems or death.

d. Everted Laryngeal Saccules (EVS)

EVS is inside-out tissue blocking the throat. It is the earliest stage of a collapsing larynx and is treated with surgery to prevent suffocation. It is detected from snoring, congestion, or shortness of breath. Owners must observe symptoms early to fix problems before they develop more.

e. Stenotic Nares

This is the official name for narrow nostrils. Having this is essentially like breathing through a straw. As with the other respiratory disorders, blue gums, fainting, or heat intolerance can be alerting factors. This can be fixed by surgically removing the tissue blockage so the dog can live a healthy life.

2. *Heart*

a. Aortic Stenosis

This is the shrinking of the main artery from the heart. It is developed at birth and needs open heart surgery and heart-lung bypass surgery to treat it. It can also be developed in dogs with bad immune systems. Keep an eye out for a heart murmur, congestive heart failure, and fainting as precursors.

3. *Eyes*

a. Entropion

This is a genetic disorder and is represented by flipped eyelids. This can lead to irritation or scar tissue accumulation causing decreased visual ability. Be on the lookout for mucous or pus, tears, or swollen eyes. Entropion can be cured with antibiotics, eye drops, or surgery.

b. Keratoconjunctivitis Sicca (KCS)

This is more commonly known as dry eye, and is caused by an immune disorder, virus, hypothyroidism, or even some medications. It will make your dog's eyes burn and become hard to keep open. Fortunately, as long as you are proactive with eye drops and medicine, there is little permanent harm to your dog.

c. Pigmentary Keratitis (PK)

Due to facial features once again, this is a deposit of pigment on the eye in a brown or black color. Most likely a genetic condition, most eye diseases can trigger this. It is found by visible recognition, excessive blinking, or dry eyes. It is cured primarily by surgery.

d. Progressive Retinal Atrophy (PRA)

This is the slow blinding of your dog. It can either happy very early in life from abnormal cells, or very late as degenerating cells. There is no pain, but it can lead to a lifetime of struggle for you and your dog. Check for light response and pupil dilation frequently to observe if your dog has PRA.

4. *Knees*

a. Luxating Patella

This is dislocation of the kneecap. Oftentimes it is the result of arthritis and can be easily observed by limping or unusual movement in the back legs. Ninety percent of the time, surgery can fully fix this.

5. *Brain*

a. Encephalitis

This is a strange disorder of brain inflammation. It is thought to be an auto-immune disorder, where the body attacks itself. If your dog stumbles, has seizures, becomes blind, experiences pain, or otherwise acts strangely, get them checked. Fatality is common, but new drugs show potential to benefit pup's lives.

Prevention & Monitoring

Beyond genetic issues (something you should learn about the parents before getting your puppy), the problem you have to worry about is weight. Previous chapters provide information about the right diet and exercise for your Pug. Refraining from giving your Pug foods made of grains and keeping his daily caloric intake within a healthy range area are essential given the dog's size. Considering the fact that he will eat whatever you give him, your dog's weight is always going to be a concern if you aren't careful. Your vet will likely talk to you if your dog has too much weight on its body because this not only puts a strain on the dog's legs, joints, and muscles, but it can have adverse effects on your dog's heart, blood flow, and respiratory system.

CHAPTER 18.
Your Aging Pug

Pugs have a life expectancy of between 12 and 15 years. They are prone to some late-in-life problems, like hip dysplasia, that will mean making some real changes in your life as your dog reaches the golden years. A senior Pug is nine years old and up. As your dog ages, you will need to start making adjustments to accommodate his or her reduced abilities. A dog may remain healthy his or her entire life, but the body just won't be able to do the same activities at 12 that it could do at two. The changes you need to make will be based on your Pug's specific needs. The decline tends to be gradual, just little things here and there, like your Pug having less traction on smooth surfaces. Over time, the body will start to deteriorate so that your dog will not be able to jump as high.

As your Pug's energy and abilities decrease, you need to make sure that he or she is not overdoing it. You should always make sure your dog doesn't over-exercise, but this is even more important for an older dog. Pugs may be too focused on having fun to realize they are hurting until they start to rest. These later years will be just as much fun; you will just need to make sure your Pug isn't pushing the new limitations. It is easy to make the senior years incredibly enjoyable for your Pug and yourself by making the necessary adjustments that allow your dog to keep being active without overexertion.

Photo Courtesy of Lam Cao

Senior Dog Care

It is usually easier to take care of a senior dog than a young dog, and the Pug is no exception. Naps are just as exciting as walks. Sleeping beside you while you watch television, or even if you nap with your dog is pretty much all it takes to make your Pug happy (though that was probably true when he was young too).

However, you must continue to be vigilant about diet and exercise. Now is not the time to let your Pug start to eat anything and everything or to neglect to take your regular walks. A senior Pug cannot handle extra weight, so you must be careful to ensure he or she remains healthy with age.

HELPFUL TIP
The Golden Years

With good nutrition, frequent exercise, excellent veterinary care, and lots of love your pug should live a long and healthy life. As with people, aging is a gradual process. You may notice your pug slowing down and having trouble climbing up or going down stairs because of arthritis. You can be proactive about eventual hearing loss in your pet by teaching him hand signals along with verbal commands. Man is a dog's best friend. Advocate on behalf of your pet so he can age with dignity.

If your canine cannot manage long walks, make the walks shorter and more numerous and spend more time romping around your yard or home.

When it comes to items that your Pug will need to access regularly, you should make some changes to your current configuration.

- Set water bowls out in a couple of different places so that your dog can easily reach them as needed. If your Pug shows signs of having trouble drinking or eating, you can place slightly raised water dishes around the home to make it easier for him to drink.

- Cover hard floor surfaces (such as tiles, hardwood, and vinyl). Use carpets or rugs that will not slip out from under your Pug.

- Add cushions and softer bedding for your Pug. This will both make the surface more comfortable and help your Pug stay warmer. There are some bed warmers for dogs if your Pug displays achy joints or muscles often. Of course, you also need to make sure your Pug isn't too warm, so this can be a fine balancing act.

- Increase how often you brush your Pug to improve his or her circulation. This should be very agreeable to your Pug as a way to make

Photo Courtesy of
Karsten & Nikita Engelbrecht

up for other limitations that means you can do other activities less often.

- Stay inside in extreme heat and cold. Your Pug is hardy, but the old canine body cannot handle the extreme changes as well as once it did.

- Use stairs or ramps for your Pug instead of constantly picking up your canine. Picking your Pug up may be more convenient for you, but it is not healthy for you or your Pug. Let your dog maintain a bit more self-sufficiency.

- Avoid changing your furniture around, particularly if your Pug shows signs of having trouble with his or her sight. A familiar home is more comforting and less stressful as your pet ages. If your Pug is not able to see as clearly as he or she once did, keeping the home familiar will make it easier for your dog to move around without getting hurt.

- If you have stairs, consider setting up an area where your dog can stay without having to use the stairs as often.

- Create a space where your Pug can relax with fewer distractions and noises. Your Pug will probably be even less comfortable being left alone for extended periods, but you should have a place where you and your older dog can just relax without loud or startling noises. Don't make your little friend feel isolated, but do give him or her a place to get away from everyone if he needs to be alone.

- Be prepared to let your dog out more often for restroom breaks.

Nutrition

Since a decrease in exercise is inevitable for any aging dog, you will need to adjust your pet's diet. If you opt to feed your Pug commercial dog food, make sure you change to the senior food. If you make your Pug's food, take the time to research how best to reduce calories without sacrificing taste. Your canine is going to need less fat in his or her food, so you may need to find something healthier that still has a lot taste to supplement the types of foods you gave your Pug as a puppy or active adult dog.

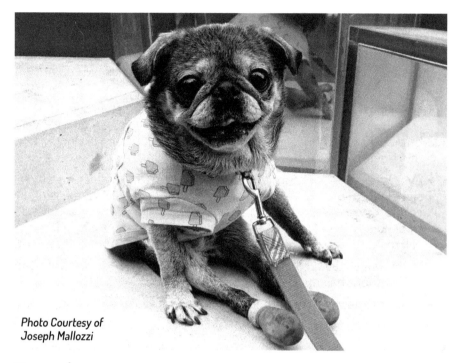

*Photo Courtesy of
Joseph Mallozzi*

Exercise

Exercise will be entirely up to you because your Pug is still just happy to be with you. If you make fewer demands, decrease the number of walks, or in any way change the routine, your Pug will quickly adapt to the new program. It is up to you to adjust the schedule and keep your Pug happily active. Usually, increasing the number of walks with shorter durations will help keep your Pug as active as necessary.

Keep in mind that your Pug is more likely to gain weight in the later years, something that his or her body really cannot handle. While the exercise will be reduced, it should not be eliminated. Keep to what your dog can manage and adjust food accordingly to keep the weight healthy.

This will probably be the hardest part of watching your Pug age. However, you will need to watch your Pug for signs of tiredness or pain so that you can stop exercising before your dog has done too much. Your pace will need to be slower and your attention more on your dog, but ultimately it can be just as exciting. You will probably notice that your Pug spends more time sniffing. This could be a sign that your dog is tiring, or it could be his or her way of acknowledging that long steady walks are a thing of the past and he is stopping to enjoy the little things more. It is an interesting time and gives you a chance to get to understand your Pug as the years start to show. Your Pug may also let you know that it is time to go home by turning around to go back or sitting down a lot and looking at you. Take the hint and go home if your Pug lets you know that the limit has been reached.

Mental Stimulation

Unlike the body, your Pug's mind is usually going to be just as sharp and clever in the golden years. That means you can start making adjustments to focus more on the activities that are mentally stimulating. You can start doing training for fun because your Pug will be just as able to learn now as when he or she was one year old. Actually, it is likely to be easier because your Pug has learned to focus better and the bond will make him happy to have something he can still do with you.

Your Pug will be grateful for the shift in focus and additional attention. Getting your senior Pug new toys is one way to help keep your dog's mind active if you do not want to train your dog or if you just don't have the time. You can then teach the Pug different names for the toys because it will be fascinating (after all, he or she will still work for praise). Whatever toys you get, make sure they are not too rough on your dog's older jaw and teeth. Tug of war may be a game of the past (you don't want to hurt the old teeth), but other games are still very much appreciated.

Hide and seek is another game that your aging Pug can manage with relative ease. Whether you hide toys or yourself, this can be a game that keeps your Pug guessing.

Regular Vet Exams

Just as humans go to visit the doctor more often as they age, you are going to need to take your dog to see your vet with greater frequency. The vet can make sure that your Pug is staying active without being too active, and that there is no unnecessary stress on your older dog. If your canine has sustained an injury and hidden it from you, your vet is more likely to detect it.

Your vet can also make recommendations about activities and changes to your schedule based on your Pug's physical abilities and any changes in personality. For example, if your Pug is panting more now, it could be a sign of pain from stiffness. This could be difficult to distinguish given how much Pugs pant as a rule, but if you see other signs of pain, schedule a visit with the vet. Your vet can help you determine the best way to keep your Pug happy and active during the later years.

Common Old-Age Aliments

Chapters 4 and 17 cover the illnesses that are common or likely with a Pug, but old age tends to bring a slew of ailments that are not particular to any one breed. Here are the things you will need to watch for (as well as talking to your vet about them).

- Diabetes is probably the greatest concern for a breed that loves to eat as much as your Pug does, especially because he has such a small frame. Although it is usually thought of as a genetic condition, any Pug can become diabetic if not fed and exercised properly. It is another reason why it is so important to be careful with your Pug's diet and exercise levels.

- Arthritis is probably the most common ailment in any dog breed, and the Pug is no exception. If your dog is showing signs of stiffness and pain after normal activities, it is very likely that he or she has arthritis. Talk with your vet about safe ways to help minimize the pain and discomfort of this common joint ailment.

- Gum disease is a common issue in older dogs as well, and you should be just as vigilant about brushing teeth when your dog gets older as you do at any other age. A regular check on your Pug's teeth and gums can help ensure this is not a problem.

- Loss of eyesight or blindness is relatively common in older dogs, just as it is in humans. Unlike humans, however, dogs don't do well with wearing glasses. Have your dog's vision checked at least once a year and more often if it is obvious that his or her eyesight is failing. Those large eyes will need extra attention.

- Kidney disease is a common problem in older dogs and one that you should monitor for the older your Pug gets. If your canine is drinking more often and having accidents regularly, this could be a sign of something more serious than just aging. If you notice this happening, get your Pug to the vet as soon as possible and have him or her checked for kidney disease.

Enjoying the Final Years

The last years of your Pug's life can actually be just as enjoyable (if not more so) than earlier stages. The energy and activities that the two of you used to do will be replaced with more attention and relaxation than at any other time. Finally having your Pug be calm enough to just sit still and enjoy your company can be incredibly nice (just remember to keep up his or her activity levels instead of getting too complacent with your Pug's newfound love of resting and relaxing).

Steps and Ramps

Pugs are small, but that does not mean that you should be picking them up more often as they age. Picking up your dog more often can do even more physical harm. There are two good reasons to ensure your Pug is able to move around without you picking him or her up.

- Having an older body means he is fragile and should not be picked up to avoid unnecessary pain.
- Independence in movement is best for you and your Pug. You do not want your Pug to come to expect you to pick him up every time he wants to get on the furniture or into the car.

Steps and ramps are the best way to ensure your Pug can keep some level of self-sufficiency. Also, you don't want to spoil your Pug in the later years. Using steps and ramps provides a bit of different activity that can work as a way of getting a bit of extra exercise.

Enjoy the Advantages

A Pug can be just as much fun in old age because his favorite thing is being with you. Your pet is just as mischievous as during the early years but has learned to chill a bit more.

Your pet will find the warmest and most comfortable places and will want you to join him or her. Your dog is incredibly devoted and will be happy to just share a short stroll followed by a lazy evening at home.

What to Expect

Your Pug probably isn't going to suffer from fear that you are less interested in spending time together. He or she will continue be the loving mischief-maker at every opportunity—that does not change with age. Just how much he can do changes. Your canine's limitations should dictate interactions and activities. If you are busy, make sure you schedule time with your Pug to do things that are within those limitations. Your happiness is still of utmost importance to your dog, so let the little canine know you feel the same way about his or her happiness. It is just as easy to make an older Pug happy as it is with a young one, and it is easier on you since relaxing is more essential.

CPSIA information can be obtained
at www.ICGtesting.com
Printed in the USA
LVHW060813140322
713354LV00003BB/4